Discover the world's best destinations with the Insight Guides app, available to download for free in the App Store and Google Play.

The container app provides easy access to fantastic free content on events and activities taking place in your current location or chosen destination, with the possibility of booking, as well as the regularly-updated Insight Guides travel blog: Inspire Me. In addition, you can purchase curated, premium destination guides through the app, which feature local highlights, hotel, bar, restaurant and shopping listings, an A to Z of practical information and more. Or purchase and download Insight Guides eBooks straight to your device.

INSIGHT ⊙ GUIDES

Walking Eye

⊙ DESTINATIONS

⊘ INSPIRE ME

☷ EBOOKS

▦ EVENTS

TOP 10 ATTRACTIONS

L'AVENTURE DU SUCRE MUSEUM
Get a taste of the island's sugar-producing heritage at this fascinating museum. See page 46.

BELLE MARE BEACH
The stuff of daydreams: white sand, palm trees and warm, turquoise waters. See page 47.

KESTREL VALLEY
Its forests and trails beckon nature-lovers. See page 50.

BLACK RIVER GORGES NATIONAL PARK
Dramatic mountain vistas unfold. See page 53.

LE GRIS GRIS
Huge waves crash against a wild coast.
See page 59.

CHAMAREL WATERFALLS
This dramatic cataract tumbles from the mountains. See page 54.

FRANÇOIS LEGUAT GIANT TORTOISE AND CAVE RESERVE
See endemic plants and a colony of giant tortoises in Rodrigues. See page 80.

ÎLE AUX CERFS
Clear waters off this tiny island make for great snorkelling. See page 47.

SIR SEEWOOSAGUR RAMGOOLAM BOTANIC GARDENS
An impressive showcase for tropical plants.
See page 45.

EUREKA MANSION
A handsome colonial gem in a tropical garden setting.
See page 37.

A PERFECT DAY

9.00am

Breakfast

Get off to a good start, away from the hustle and bustle of town, with a full English breakfast at Lambic in St Georges Street. If it's fine you can sit outside under the shade of the mango trees and sip your coffee.

10.00am

Green spaces

Walk breakfast off with a stroll through Company Gardens, see the Royal Palms in Place d'Armes leading up to Government House or people-watch in Bowen Gardens.

2.00pm

Retail therapy

Make your way to Farquhar Street and test your haggling skills with pavement vendors before browsing for souvenirs in the Central Market. For fixed-price shopping take the underpass to the Caudan Waterfront and hit the Craft Market and scores of speciality shops.

12.00pm

Colonial chic

Take in the colonial architecture nearby, the Treasury Buildings and Municipal Theatre, before a light lunch of Lebanese appetizers at Le Sultan.

4.00pm

Stamp duty

Check out the Blue Penny Museum nearby for famous portraits, fine art and philately. Cool off with a long drink on the terrace of the Labourdonnais Hotel or head to the Food Court for fast food options.

6.30pm

Dinner
Visit Le Courtyard, an elegant restaurant at the corner of St Louis and Chevreau Streets (see page 108), with a shady terrace and a location in the heart of this bustling city. Taste wonderful dishes bursting with the flavours of France and Mauritius.

10.00pm

On the town
Try your luck on blackjack, roulette and poker tables at the Casino or prop up the bar until the last punter leaves. Otherwise plenty of taxis are on hand to take you north to the clubs and bars at Grand Baie. Best of the bunch is Banana Beach Club (tel: 230 263 0326), a trusted hangout for live music by local jazz, rock and blues artistes.

5.30pm

Sundowner
Take a free water taxi from the jetty car park across Bassin des Chaloupes to the trendy Spinnaker's Bar at Le Suffren Hotel, order a Green Island rum cocktail and catch a magnificent sunset from the terrace.

8.30pm

Bollywood versus Hollywood
Catch the latest English-subtitled Bollywood movies at the Cinema Klassic (tel: 230 213 4831) or settle for a French-dubbed Hollywood blockbuster at The Star Cinema Complex (tel: 230 211 6866) in the Caudan.

CONTENTS

INTRODUCTION

Mauritius has long entranced its visitors. Charles Baudelaire called it 'the perfumed land, fondled by the sun', while Mark Twain noted simply that 'heaven was copied after Mauritius'. The stunning white, sandy beaches lapped by aquamarine seas earn every superlative, and thousands of modern visitors to Mauritius agree that this tiny dot in the Indian Ocean is the stuff of desert-island dreams. With much of its coastline fringed by coral reef, a landscape set off by diminutive mountains, temperatures rarely falling below 20°C (68°F) and some of the world's finest hotels, Mauritius is a perfect year-round holiday destination.

But there is more to Mauritius than the exclusive beachside hotels that have come to be the regular haunt of celebrities and big-spenders. Stray inland and you will

Mauritian women with temple offerings

discover mountains, for-
ests, rivers and waterfalls,
fields undulating with sugar
cane, extinct volcanic craters, tumbledown towns
and villages, and hospitable
locals.

LOCATION

Mauritius lies 805km (500
miles) east of Madagascar,
one of a trio of islands, along
with Rodrigues and Réunion,
known as the Mascarenes.

Rochester Falls

Shaped like a pear, Mauritius
covers an area of 1,865 sq km (720 sq miles). The island forms
the main component of the Republic of Mauritius, which also
includes the much smaller islands of Agalega and St Brandon
in the Carados Carajos group and the semi-autonomous
island of Rodrigues.

There are three mountain ranges, courtesy of a volcanic
past: the Moka range forms an amphitheatre around the
capital Port Louis; the Black River chain occupies the
southwest, merging with the Savanne mountains in the
extreme south; and the Grand Port range lies in the southeast. Along the coast, the beaches, resorts and hotels of
the north attract the majority of visitors; the west, with its
fantastic sunsets and access to rugged inland areas, is fast
catching up; the east is isolated and rural, but has some
very luxurious hotels; the remote south is in the early
stages of development.

The rare pink pigeon

THE PEOPLE

There are no indigenous people. The 1.3 million islanders are the descendants of African slaves, indentured Indian labourers and Chinese traders, resulting in all shades of skin colour, a living legacy of over 300 years of colonisation by the French and British. On this, one of the most densely populated islands on Earth, Indo-Mauritians form the majority at 68 percent, followed by Creoles or people of mixed European or African origin at 27 percent, Sino-Mauritians at 3 percent and white Franco-Mauritians at 2 percent. In Rodrigues there are some 39,000 islanders, predominantly of Creole-African descent. For most of the time the republic's multicultural inhabitants get along in remarkable harmony.

Travelling round Mauritius reveals a naturally friendly people who are keen to help visitors. Many live in the crowded plateau towns of Curepipe, Floreal, Rose Hill–Beau Bassin, and Quatre Bornes in the centre of the island and in small villages. It is here that you discover the islanders' strong adherence to cultural traditions, witness religious festivals, taste a cuisine as diverse as its people and hear a multitude of different languages, including Creole, French, Hindi, Bhojpuri and, to a lesser degree,

English, in an environment that contrasts so strongly with the luxurious beach hotels and bustling tourist resorts of Grand Baie, Pereybere and Flic-en-Flac.

FLORA AND FAUNA

Three hundred years of human settlement has greatly altered the vegetation and wildlife of Mauritius. Little remains of the original flora other than a few patches of forest, declared as nature reserves, in the centre of the island and on some offshore islands. The demise of the dodo in the 17th century (see page 19) is only the most publicised extinction of the island's birdlife. Now only seven species of endemic birds remain, the most noted being the

CREOLE

Creole is a language that was originally created by the need for French plantation masters to communicate with their slaves, and for the slaves, who often spoke different dialects, to understand each other. Creole became the island's *lingua franca*. Continuously modified by years of French and English colonisation, Indian immigration and Chinese settlers, it has become a hopelessly corrupted language that often confuses Mauritians themselves. Full of imagery and nuances, it is slightly easier to understand if you have a basic knowledge of French.

As a visitor staying in the tourist resorts you will get by without any difficulty speaking English or French, but in informal situations a few Creole expressions, such as *li bon* (that's good/fine) or *ki maniere* (how are you) or *tout correk* (OK), are always appreciated. If you're in Mauritian company, you'll find that the conversation may take place in Creole, French or English or a combination of all three.

Mauritius kestrel, the pink pigeon and the echo parakeet. These birds can be seen in the Black River Gorges, while the pink pigeon now thrives on Île aux Aigrettes Nature Reserve off Mahébourg.

Imported fauna include deer, monkey, the tendrec (a tailless hedgehog), mongoose and the wild boar. There are three species of gecko, several tree lizards and the couleuvre, a non-poisonous snake from India. Wildlife is generally harmless, although extra care should be taken to avoid stepping on stonefish, whose spines can inflict serious injury.

SUGAR, TOURISM AND BEYOND

Many fruits and vegetables and small amounts of coffee are grown for home consumption, although rice, a staple food, has to be imported in large quantities from Asia. Sugar cane is the dominant crop. Great tracts of it swathe the island,

The vibrant red of the flame tree

giving the land a fresh, green tropical appearance virtually year round.

Sugar production, once the island's most important industry, has given way to tourism and textile manufacturing, bringing Mauritius much-needed foreign income. While the impact of international terrorism and weather phenomena in Asia has, so far, had little effect on tourist numbers, increasing competition coupled with a fall in demand and the global recession has resulted in the closure of many textile factories. In spite of this setback, economic diversification continues. Mauritius promotes itself as an offshore banking centre, and a scheme to transform Mauritius into a 'cyber island' is almost complete, with the construction of several centres of business process outsourcing occupied by major foreign companies.

Blue skies and Mount Brabant on the horizon

Mauritius is taking its first steps into 'green tourism', with inland activities – such as rock-climbing, soft safaris, nature walks, quad-biking, canyoning and mountain-biking – now available on land owned by the sugar estates. Such excursions make a welcome change from the beach, revealing a multi-faceted island. Meanwhile, luxury spa and golf resorts and eco-lodges, on the fast-developing south coast in particular, continue to grow. These new ventures, together with a surge in more affordable accommodation and the introduction of an open-skies policy, make the island more than just a holiday dream.

A BRIEF HISTORY

Eight million years ago, Mauritius rose from the depths of the southwestern Indian Ocean in a series of volcanic eruptions. Réunion and Rodrigues followed a couple of million years later. These three islands are today known as the Mascarenes, after Portuguese Admiral, Pedro Mascarenhas, who visited the area in 1513.

The volcanic activity carved out a distinctive landscape of mountains, craters and coastal plains; lagoons and reefs were later additions. Trees and other plant life gradually covered the Mascarenes, which became the exclusive preserve of millions of birds attracted to a sea teeming with marine life. Prominent bird species included the flightless dodo of Mauritius and the solitaire of Rodrigues. Human occupation was to lead to the extinction of these species and the decimation of indigenous forests.

EARLY SETTLERS

Early 15th-century Arab maps show Mauritius as Dina Arobi and Rodrigues as Dina Moraze, but there is no evidence that Arab explorers ever settled on either island. The first European visitors were the Portuguese in the early 16th century, who named Rodrigues after the navigator, Diego Rodriguez, and christened Mauritius after his ship the *Cirne*, Ilha do Cirne. Later Portuguese explorers and traders used the islands as convenient bases on the long voyages between the Cape of Good Hope and India but, like the Arabs, they never settled. They did leave a lasting legacy, however, by deliberately introducing cattle and monkeys so that there would be fresh meat supplies when ships called. These introduced animals, including rats and dogs escaping from ships, upset the delicate ecological balance that had existed for millions of years. In about 1539 the last Portuguese sailors left Mauritius and the island was unoccupied for more than 50 years, save for occasional visits by pirates who roamed the Indian Ocean.

ARRIVAL OF THE DUTCH

The Dutch arrived in 1598, landing in the southeast of Mauritius at Vieux Grand Port, a natural harbour near present-day Mahébourg, and named the island after Prince Maurice of Nassau. They built a fort, the remains of which were excavated in 1997, and settled along the coast where they planted crops – including sugar cane – and began to cut down the ebony forests for export. With the French and British vying for this valuable commodity, the settlers realised that the harbour in the northwest was vulnerable to invasion and sent a small detachment of troops to what is the present capital, Port Louis. But cyclones, drought, food shortages and quarrels among settlers led to a Dutch withdrawal from the island in 1658.

Early 18th-century map

In 1664 another attempt at colonisation was made when the Dutch East India Company, based in Batavia (present-day Jakarta, Indonesia) realised the strategic importance of Mauritius in the context of the sea route between Europe and the Indies. The new settlers cleared more ebony forests, introduced deer to overcome food shortages and imported

The extinct dodo

slaves from Madagascar and convicts from southeast Asia to work the fields. But apathy, an overall inefficient administration and attacks by pirates forced them to leave the island for good in 1710. All that was left was a group of runaway slaves. The only humans who came ashore were crews of visiting ships, and pirates who had established their own republic, Libertalia, in Madagascar in 1685. The pirates targeted the expanding maritime trade route between Europe and the Indies, raiding the ships of the various East India companies.

FRENCH COLONISATION
Soon after the Dutch left, the French arrived in 1715, took possession of the island and renamed it Île de France. The first French colonists landed at Mahébourg in 1722, but dangerous reefs and contrary winds threatened their ships, so they moved to the safety of Port Louis. Piracy continued throughout the French period. The French issued Letters of Marque to pirates and owners of private ships, authorising

them to attack foreign ships in the name of France. The holders of these letters became known as corsairs or privateers.

In 1735 Bertrand François Mahé de Labourdonnais, a naval officer, arrived at Port Louis as the new governor of the Mascarene Islands and set about transforming Île de France into a flourishing colony. A large labour force was crucial to his plans, and he began the importation of thousands of slaves from Africa and Madagascar. Ships were built, farms improved, roads constructed, and forests cut down to make way for sugar plantations. With French supremacy now well established in the Indian Ocean, the French East India Company supplied ships and stores to Port Louis for campaigns against the British in India.

In 1767 the company suffered heavy financial losses following the defeat of the French by the British in India. Labourdonnais was falsely accused of bribery and thrown into prison; Île de France was handed over to the crown. The French Revolution of 1789 had little effect on the islanders and if anything the influence of new ideas manifested itself in

THE DEMISE OF THE DODO

Mauritius' best-known indigenous bird, the dodo, is the world's most famous example of extinction and a symbol of man's destructiveness. The bird was fat, friendly and flightless. Clumsy and tame to the point of foolishness, this 23kg (50lb) bird made easy prey for the first Dutch settlers when they arrived in the early 17th century; they killed thousands of dodos for their meat. At the same time, the bird's eggs and chicks made tasty morsels for introduced animals, such as rats, monkeys and dogs. Some live dodos were taken to Europe and shown off as the greatest living freaks of the day. By the late 17th century, however, there were no more dodos to show off – the species had become extinct.

a wave of loose living. The elite, bound by their common belief in slavery, had their own revolution when in 1796, France sent two officials to announce the news that slavery would be abolished. The colonists' fervour for liberty, equality and fraternity wore thin and the officials, amid rioting and unrest, were promptly sent back home.

Conflict with the British intensified, with the French using corsairs to attack British shipping. Between 1793 and 1802, corsairs captured more than a hundred East India ships, which were brought to Port Louis. The capital soon earned a reputation as a den of thieves where ruined adventurers, swindlers and pirates provided the corsairs with a ready outlet to dispose of stolen goods.

Île de France's period of autonomy lasted till 1803 when Napoleon appointed a new governor, General Decaen. Decaen curried favour with the elite by allowing slavery and privateering, both hugely profitable, to continue. Meanwhile, the British continued to lose valuable cargoes to the corsairs.

BRITISH COLONISATION

After months of blockading Port Louis, the British based themselves at Rodrigues and took the island of Réunion before launching a major naval attack in 1810 on Mahébourg. The four-day Battle of Grand Port ended in defeat for the British, with heavy casualties on both sides. However, a few months later, in December, a huge British fleet landed at Cap Malheureux and troops marched to Port Louis. The French offered only token resistance and Île de France became a British colony, reverting to its former name, Mauritius.

Grand victory

The 1810 Battle of Grand Port was the only French victory over the British at sea during the Napoleonic Wars. The battle's name is inscribed on the Arc de Triomphe in Paris.

Pont Etienne by Thuillier, 1847

The British capitulation terms were generous: anybody who wanted to leave could do so and were given a free passage home; while settlers were allowed to keep their laws, customs, language, religion and property, a term which included their slaves. By eliminating Mauritius as a corsair base and establishing a governor and garrison, the British achieved supremacy in the Indian Ocean. English became the official language, but the island retained much of its French character.

Under Robert Farquhar, first British governor, Port Louis became a free port, roads were built and trade flourished. Sugar production soared and the planters badly needed slaves to clear land and plant cane – despite the fact that slavery had been abolished in the British Empire in 1807. In 1832 Judge John Jeremie, the Attorney-General, arrived in Mauritius to announce abolition without compensation to hostile planters and slave owners. He was forced to leave almost immediately. In response, the British built Fort Adelaide (La Citadelle) on a hill overlooking Port Louis to quell demonstrations. Slavery was finally abolished in 1835.

Britain turned to the Indian subcontinent for cheap labour to maintain sugar production. During the 19th century, nearly half a million Indians arrived at the Aapravasi Ghat in Port

Indian labourers

Louis, many in conditions not far short of slavery. They were paid a pittance, worked long hours and often subjected to harsh treatment.

In 1872 a Royal Commission was appointed to look into the problems of Indian immigration. The Indians' living standards improved slightly and immigration was finally halted in 1909, when another Royal Commission made recommendations for social and political reform. By now many Indians had settled in Mauritius; today their descendants form the majority of the population.

In 1936 the Indians took political action and campaigned for better working conditions. Strikes the following year and again in 1943 brought the sugar industry to a standstill. The British responded by drawing up plans for constitutional reform. But the real turning point came in 1959 when the first elections under universal suffrage were held. They were won by the Labour Party under a Hindu doctor, Seewoosagur Ramgoolam (who was later knighted).

INDEPENDENCE

In 1968 Britain agreed to grant independence on condition that the British take over the Chagos Archipelago, a group of islands 1,930km (1,200 miles) northeast of Mauritius. These islands, inhabited by the *ilois* or islanders, had been part of the British colony of Mauritius since 1814, when France ceded them to Britain. In 1965, a secret deal was made between Britain and the United States whereby in exchange for leasing one of the islands in the group, Diego Garcia, for 50 years, the British Government would get a discount of $11 million on Polaris submarines. The islands were then detached from Mauritius and became part of the new British Indian Ocean Territory (BIOT). The *ilois* were displaced and taken to Mauritius where they were dumped at the docks and left to fend for themselves. Diego Garcia is now a major US military base, off limits to all. Whether the *ilois* will ever return to their homeland seems nothing but a distant dream.

In the run-up to independence fears arose that politics would become 'Indianised', and many Mauritians settled abroad. In 1968 Sir Seewoosagur Ramgoolam became the first prime minister.

In the early 1980s, following a series of corruption scandals, high unemployment and over-population problems, the opposition party, the MMM, swept into power. After that came several governments that were coalitions of the four major parties.

In 1992 Mauritius became an independent republic within the Commonwealth. The Queen was replaced as head of state by a locally nominated president.

A nation's father

The first prime minister of Mauritius, Sir Seewoosagur Ramgoolam (1900–85), became known as 'the Father of the Nation'. The Royal Botanic Gardens at Pamplemousses were renamed in his honour two years after his death.

MODERN MAURITIUS

Harvesting sugar cane

Since independence, the island's dependence on sugar has lessened. Manufacturing and textile industries rose in importance from the 1970s, but today the country's main markets for manufactured goods are turning to cheaper sources elsewhere. Many textile factories have closed and unemployment is around 7.5 percent.

Sugar production, while still a major pillar of the economy, no longer employs the huge numbers it used to. Changes to international sugar pricing agreements have hit the industry hard, and sugar barons are turning their lands over to real-estate development and tourism.

Tourism remains the major foreign income earner. Luxurious golf and spa resorts, and eco-tourism attractions, such as the Ferney Valley Forest and Wildlife Reserve and Domaine du Bel Ombre, are attempts by the industry to show visitors another facet of the island beyond the sea and beaches.

'Paradise Island' it may be for those who come for the magnificent beaches, but it may not be too long before Mauritius is better known as Cyber Island. In 2005 the country launched itself into information and communications technology with the opening of Cyber City. This complex in the centre of the island, the result of Indian expertise and financial backing, has already attracted foreign companies involved in call centres and business process outsourcing. New jobs are being created to replace those lost in other sectors. Still a work in progress, only time will tell if this ambitious scheme can succeed.

HISTORICAL LANDMARKS

15th century Arab names of Dina Arobi and Dina Moraze for Mauritius and Rodrigues appear on early maps.

1513 The Mascarene Islands are named after Portuguese navigator, Pedro Mascarenhas.

1528 Diego Rodriguez, Portuguese seaman, visits Rodrigues and gives the island his name.

1598 First Dutch landing at Port South East.

1638–1710 Dutch settle in Mauritius but abandon it after several attempts to colonise. First slaves imported from Madagascar. Sugar cane, deer, pigs from Java introduced.

1691–93 Rodrigues first settled by François Leguat and nine others.

1715 French annex Mauritius, naming it Île de France.

1721–1810 French occupation. Slaves imported in huge numbers.

1735 Labourdonnais becomes first governor of the Mascarene Islands.

1793–1805 Privateering causes large losses to British East India Company. French Revolution and Napoleonic Wars provoke revolutionary fervour in Mauritius.

1810 British take Île de France and rename it Mauritius.

1814 Treaty of Paris places Mauritius, Rodrigues and the Seychelles under British ownership; Réunion is handed back to the French.

1835 Slavery abolished and replaced by Indian indentured labour.

1909 Indian immigration ceases. Royal Commission appointed to make recommendations for political and social reform.

1968 Independence from Britain. Rodrigues becomes a dependency of Mauritius. Sir Seewoosagur Ramgoolam is prime minister.

1992 Republic of Mauritius declared.

2002 Rodrigues granted regional autonomy.

2005 Opening of Cyber Tower I at Ebene; Navin Ramgoolam of the Social Alliance elected prime minister.

2014 General elections won by Alliance Lepep. Sir Anerood Jugnauth becomes Prime Minister.

2015 Ameenah Gurib-Fakim inaugurated as President.

WHERE TO GO

This guide divides Mauritius into bite-size geographical chunks. Port Louis, the capital, and the plateau towns are worth a visit at least once to experience contemporary island life. The north coast (the northwest in particular) is home to the most established resorts. The more isolated east coast may be too windy for some during the winter months, but the hotels here offer pure luxury and access to lovely offshore islands. The west coast, renowned for stunning sunsets, has fine diving and water sports and is within easy reach of the rugged Black River Gorges, as is the developing south coast. The small island of Rodrigues, a newcomer to tourism, offers a total contrast to Mauritius, with simple hotels, rugged land-scapes and a predominantly Afro-Creole population.

PORT LOUIS

In 1735 Bertrand François Mahé de Labourdonnais, the Governor-General of the Mascarene Islands, founded this settlement on the northwest coast. With 150,000 residents crammed into less than 10 sq km (4 sq miles) and thousands of workers who arrive daily from nearby, it's no surprise that **Port Louis ❶**, like most capitals, is crowded, dirty and noisy. It is devoid of any real architectural wonders and makes no claim to urban chic, but its fascination lies in its jumble of Franco-British colonial buildings juxtaposed against mod-ern office blocks and a hotchpotch of tumbledown shops and stores dwarfed by modern mini-skyscrapers.

Surrounding the city are the picturesque peaks and knolls of the Moka Mountains, including the distinct thumb-shaped Le Pouce, the tapered pinnacle of Pieter Both, named after the Dutch admiral who drowned nearby, and the huge bulk

The colourful Central Market in Port Louis

of Signal Mountain to the south. It's an atmospheric city with statues and monuments shaded by palm trees, colourful Chinese and Indian temples and churches, and a bustling market and modern waterfront. The often debilitating summer humidity reminds you that you are in the tropics.

If you are heading from the airport to one of the archetypal beach hotels in the north, your first glimpse of the capital will be from the traffic-infested dual carriageway, locally referred to as the 'motorway', which divides the old commercial district from the waterfront. Every visitor should try to spend at least a morning exploring the back streets of Port Louis with its tiny 'hole in the wall' shops, bargaining in the market and eating on the hoof along with the lunchtime crowds. Apart from the Caudan Waterfront, it's not a city that stays awake after dark.

THE WATERFRONT
Built in 1996 to replace the old harbour, the pedestrianised **Caudan Waterfront** Ⓐ complex has become the focal point of the capital. Its two modern hotels, a 24-hour casino, designer

THE MAURITIAN FLAG

Port Louis is at its most colourful on Independence Day, held on 12 March, when Government House and other public buildings are festooned with the national flag. The Mauritian flag consists of four horizontal coloured bands in red, blue, yellow and green. Officially red represents freedom and independence, blue is for the sea, yellow is for the lights of independence shining over the nation and green for the swathes of sugar cane that are so characteristic of the country. Others maintain that it reflects the island's multi-faith community: red is for the followers of Hinduism, blue for the Catholic community, yellow for the Tamils and green for the Muslims.

The Caudan Waterfront

boutiques, restaurants and businesses are housed in renovated coaster sheds and dockside buildings. In spite of recent developments, the sights of the harbour remind you that this is a working port: the industrial landscape of docks and quays includes the squat, solid red-brick Granary building (now a car park), the spruced-up Bulk Sugar Terminal, as well as cargo ships.

In 1847 Mauritius became the fifth country in the world to issue postage stamps (see page 68); the very first stamps – the Mauritian Two Penny Blue and One Penny Orange-Red – are now extremely valuable. This philatelic history is on display to the south of the waterfront in the **Blue Penny Museum** B (Mon–Sat 10am–5pm; charge; tel: 230 210 9204). The philately exhibits include examples of both stamps, and there are fine artworks, old maps, coins, postcards and historic photographs as well.

To the north, behind a smart arcade of souvenir shops, is the **Windmill Museum** (Mon–Fri 10am–noon, 1–3pm; free), which is a reconstruction of the original flour mill built by the French

Indian influx

Within a decade of the first immigrants from India in 1834, half a million more arrived, making Mauritius the British Empire's biggest recipient of Indian labour and its most successful sugar-producing colony.

in the 18th century. Inside, a collection of old photographs of Port Louis shows the transformation of the waterfront, and there are some anchors and cannon found during the renovation works. A childrens' play area provides distraction for young families.

Still on the waterfront is the colonnaded **Post Office**, built by the British in 1868, and the **Postal Museum** (Mon–Fri 9am–4.30pm, Sat until 3.30pm; charge; tel: 230 213 4812), which has a small collection of 19th-century telegraph and stamp-vending machines, postal stationery and printing plates. The museum is a good place to buy first-day covers and commemorative stamps. Nearby are the gardens of the **Aapravasi Ghat** ⓒ (Mon–Fri 9am–4pm; www.aapravasighat.org). This area used to be an immigration depot for the first indentured Indian labourers who arrived in 1834 to work on sugar estates in conditions not far removed from slavery.

In 2006 Aapravasi Ghat was given Unesco World Heritage Site status; it is recognised as the place where the 'modern indentured labour diaspora' began. Scenes of immigrant life are depicted on bronze murals.

OLD PORT LOUIS

Place d'Armes, directly opposite the waterfront, is a good place to start a tour of Old Port Louis. Here the statue of Mahé de Labourdonnais stares out to sea. Shaded by an avenue of royal palms and flanked by banks and offices, this one-way street is the heart of the capital and Port Louis' busiest thoroughfare. At the end of the street is **Government House** ⓓ, built on the site of a tumbledown wooden shack that was later enlarged by Labourdonnais as his headquarters when he transformed the city from an Indian Ocean backwater into a thriving sea port. A marble statue of Queen Victoria and, behind it, a statue of Sir William Stevenson, the British governor from 1857 to 1863, are reminders of the city's colonial past. To the right, on the corner of La Chaussée, are the former **Treasury Buildings** built in 1883, now the Prime Minister's Office, with large overhanging verandas providing respite from tropical downpours.

Along La Chaussée is the **Natural History Museum**  (Mon–Fri 9am–4pm, Sat 9am–noon. closed Wed, Sun and public holidays; free; tel: 230 210 1272), an attractive cream-coloured colonial building fronted by a huge baobab tree. Beyond the museum are **Company Gardens**, where the French East India Company had its headquarters. Today, with its bottle palms, giant banyans and statues of famous island sons, it is

Government House, Port Louis

The city's racetrack

a pleasant lunchtime setting for office workers.

The **Municipal Theatre** ❻, built in 1822 in Intendance Street, is the oldest theatre in the Indian Ocean and despite being closed until 2015 for extensive renovations, it remains a symbol of the city's culture.

Across the road from the theatre, and tucked down the cobbled lane of Rue de Vieux Conseil, is the **Museum of Photography** (Mon–Fri 10am–3pm; charge; tel: 230 211 1705). The building is crammed with impressive displays of late 19th-century photographic equipment, postcards and historical photographs of Port Louis.

City Hall and the adjacent government buildings are examples of the uninspiring concrete architecture of the 1960s, but you can't avoid them to get to the Roman Catholic **St Louis Cathedral** ❼ in Cathedral Square. This twin-towered neo-gothic cathedral, dating from 1932, is the third to be built on this site, both of its predecessors having been destroyed in cyclones. In the chapel are the remains of Madame Labourdonnais and her son. The fountain outside with its four bronze lions dates back to 1786 and provided water for city folk. Immediately behind the cathedral is the fine 19th-century colonnaded mansion of the **Episcopal Palace** with its high ceilings and wide verandas.

The cream-coloured Anglican **St James Cathedral**, hidden in tranquil Poudriere Street, occupies the site of a former gunpowder store where the French incarcerated British prisoners-of-war. The British built the single-spired cathedral in 1828 and installed a bell, which had belonged to a French governor.

At the eastern edge of Port Louis and cradled by the Moka Mountains is the **Champs de Mars** racecourse, the oldest in the southern hemisphere, best seen from the heights of **La Citadelle** ❶ (daily; charge), a now abandoned basalt-built lookout post built to the north by the British in 1832. Under the French the area was a military training ground and in 1812 it was turned into a racecourse by Colonel Edward Draper, a British army officer. Fringing the north side in Dr Eugene Laurent Street is a colourful Chinese temple bedecked with ornate scripts. For respite from the heat, make for the walking trails at **Le Dauget** in the foothills of the Moka Mountains; there are panoramic views of the city and harbour.

After 160 years of providing Port Louisiens with fresh produce from a dilapidated site between Queen and Farquhar streets, the **Central Market** ❶ relocated into an adjacent two-storey locally-built stone and timber building. All that remains of the old market are the Victorian wrought-iron gates and a meat and fish section. The new market (Mon–Sat 7am–3pm, Sun 7am–noon), which has its main entrance in Queen Street, is worth visiting for its bustling atmosphere, brash colours, strange smells and unexpected sights. You can barter for baskets, clothing, spices and even salt fish and honey, wend your way through

Built to survive

The walls of St James Anglican Cathedral were built 10ft (3m) thick to make them cyclone proof, allowing Port Louisiens to shelter inside when these fierce tropical storms struck.

In the Chinese Quarter

the fruit and vegetable stalls, or buy a herbal remedy 'guaranteed to cure all ills'. The ground floor is packed with fruit and vegetable sellers and there is an air-conditioned food section selling snacks and drinks. The upper floor has a small eating area, more souvenir stalls and great views of the market.

Perhaps the most eclectic part of the city is several blocks east of the market towards the pagoda-like entrance of **Chinatown** ❶. The air is thick with the smell of herbs and spices and the streets bristle with specialist food shops, *ayurvedic* stores, small eateries and chaotic supermarkets. Standing sentinel on the corner of Jummah Mosque Street and Royal Road is the green and white **Jummah Mosque**. Built in 1853, it is the island's most impressive mosque, with ornate teak doors and decorative walls. You will need to ask permission to visit the courtyard.

Three Chinese temples, open to the public, are some distance from Chinatown. The oldest is the **Kwan Tee Pagoda**, beside the busy roundabout south of the Caudan Waterfront, dedicated to the Chinese warrior god. Another, simply known as the **Chinese Pagoda**, is located on the corner of Generosity and Justice streets where the scent of sandalwood drifts from the red and gold interior. There is a Buddhist shrine on the first floor affording wonderful city views. The most serene is the cream-coloured **Thien Thane** temple in the verdant foothills of Signal Mountain on the southeast edge of town. Remember to remove your shoes when entering a temple.

Also on the foothills of Signal Mountain and a world away from the brouhaha of town is the peaceful setting of the shrine of **Marie Reine de la Paix**. In 1989 this place of pilgrimage was crammed with thousands of islanders gathered to hear mass said by Pope John Paul II. It is still used by the Catholic community for religious gatherings. From the wide paved walkway and lovely lawned terraces there are great views of the city and harbour.

Line Barracks , which has its public entrance in Jemmapes Street, sits squarely around a central courtyard and takes up several city blocks.

The Thien Thane temple

Built in 1764 by the last governor of the French East India Company to house troops who had previously been billeted in private homes, today it is the headquarters of the Mauritius Police Force and is arguably one of Port Louis' quirkiest sites. Learner drivers take their licence test here, gingerly steering a course round gardens containing a petrified dodo and the odd cannon or two and past the city prison dubbed 'Alcatraz', before emerging into the busy streets through an incongruous blue-tiled archway marked 'Gateway of Discipline'.

Honouring Père Laval at his shrine

OUTSIDE PORT LOUIS

The **Church and Shrine of Père Laval**, to the northeast of Port Louis in the suburb of **Sainte-Croix**, is dedicated to the French missionary, Jacques Desiré Laval, who arrived in 1841 to convert black ex-slaves to Catholicism. When Père Laval died in 1864, his special healing powers became legendary and in 1979 the Catholic Church beatified him. The modern white church replaced the original, which was damaged by Cyclone Carol in 1962, and is worth visiting for its abstract-style **stained-glass windows**, lofty convex timber ceiling and modern mosaics depicting the life of Christ. Beside the church stands a vault containing a stone sarcophagus enclosing the remains of Père Laval's body beneath an effigy framed with flowers and candles placed by people of all faiths. There is also a small shop selling postcards, books and souvenirs of a religious bent, and plenty of information in French and English on the life of Père Laval. The adjacent **presbytery** is a superb example of 19th-century colonial architecture.

South of the capital, just off the motorway at **Pailles**, is the 1,200-hectare (3,000-acre) estate of **Domaine les Pailles** (daily 10am–4.30pm; charge; tel: 230 286 4425; www.domaineles pailles.net). The estate includes a reconstruction of an early oxen-powered sugar mill, a spice garden, rum distillery and mask museum; there are also optional guided tours. Rides in a colonial-style horse-drawn carriage, jeep safaris and activities for children are also offered. Four restaurants, one with a swimming pool (see page 108), a casino and the futuristic **Swami Vivekananda Conference Centre** make the estate a popular destination for both business people and tourists.

Further south along the motorway at **Montagne Ory** is the colonial mansion called **Eureka ❷** (daily 10am–4pm; charge; tel: 230 5772 9303; www.eureka-house.com). Built in 1856 by an Englishman, it was later auctioned to the wealthy Leclezio, a Franco-Mauritian family, one of whom cried 'Eureka' when his bid was accepted. This ancestral home is now a museum. Built entirely of indigenous wood, the main house has a total of 109 doors, and the high-ceilinged rooms are filled with antique furniture that reflects a bygone era. You can take tea on the spacious veranda of the main house, explore the external stone-built kitchen equipped with original Creole cookware or take a riverside nature walk through tropical gardens towards a deep ravine and waterfall.

Eureka

THE NORTH

The coast north from Port Louis attracts the most visitors to Mauritius because of the stunning stretches of white, sandy beaches backed by turquoise lagoons, the fine hotels, and the popular resorts of Trou aux Biches, Grand Baie and Péreybère. The region also has access to a collection of off-shore islands, as well as a number of inland attractions, providing distraction for beach lovers and water-sports enthusiasts. Although hotels maintain the best beaches, no beach is private and as long as you don't access them via the hotel entrance you are free to use them.

A fast dual-lane carriageway, locally referred to as the 'motorway', links the north to Port Louis, with a series of roundabouts leading to villages and on to the various resorts.

Inland, sugar cane clothes a flat landscape broken by the gentlest of hills. From July to December when the cane is harvested, there are superb views to the south of Port Louis' Moka Mountains, which provide a natural compass from which to get your bearings if you're walking, cycling or driving. At other times of the year, the sugar cane is so high that the view is obscured and travelling is like being in a maze, although there is always somebody around to ask for directions.

NORTH FROM PORT LOUIS

A series of sheltered bays and long stretches of beach pepper the coast north of the capital. First is **Le Goulet**, an attractive white crescent of sand nestling between low cliffs and backed by a forest of casuarinas just off the Arsenal road. Next is the **Baie du Tombeau** (Bay of the Tombs) on the B29. In 1615 four ships belonging to the Dutch East India Company were caught in a cyclone, which swept them on to the reef here. Everybody drowned, including Admiral Pieter Both, after whom the Port Louis mountain peak is named.

The next bay is **Baie aux Tortues** (Turtle Bay), dominated by appealing beach hotels which flank the banks of the River Citron. Here, ammunition was supplied for French expeditions to India from an arsenal at nearby Moulin a Poudre. The bay is a designated marine park, popular with snorkellers, but the corals have been damaged by nearby hotel developments. At nearby Balaclava there are some ruins of a 19th-century private estate and a waterfall in the grounds of the Maritim Hotel.

The small village of **Pointe aux Piments** hugs the shore, revealing glimpses of local life and a lovely rocky beach backed by grassy verges dotted with religious shrines. The attractive **Aquarium** (Mon–Sat 10am–4pm, Sun and public holidays 10am–3pm; charge; tel: 230 261 4561 www.mauritiusaquarium.com) on the coast road is worth visiting for its collection of reef and lagoon fish displayed in several huge tanks.

Maheswarnath temple

Trou aux Biches, a former fishing village, has developed into a popular international resort with a proliferation of shops, supermarkets and eateries. The 3km (2 miles) of white, sandy beach includes a public beach but much is dominated by the Trou aux Biches Hotel. At nearby **Triolet** is the island's largest Hindu shrine, built in 1857, the imposing **Maheswarnath Temple**. In return for a guided tour, you may be asked for a donation, which you should place directly into the sealed box at the entrance.

The most popular public beach is further north at **Mon Choisy ❸**. Here, a grassy football pitch, a former landing strip, is marked with a monument commemorating the first flight from Mauritius to Réunion in 1933 by two French pilots, Hily and Surtel. At weekends the blindingly white beach is crammed with campers in makeshift tents and families feasting on *farathas* and curries; impromptu *sega* dances take place beneath the shade of a dense casuarina forest. Mid-week it is an ideal location for snorkelling, swimming, strolling or horse-riding. At the back of the beach, **Horse Riding Delights**, a former 19th-century sugar estate that is now a leisure park (tel: 230 265 6159, reservations only), offers guided tours of the ruins and an insight into how sugar shaped the economy of the island.

Pointe aux Canonniers (Gunners Point), reached through an avenue of flamboyant trees from Mon Choisy, is an historic headland. The French used it as a garrison and shore battery and the British as a military and quarantine post. Today, this is a tranquil coastline indented with pristine beaches, and the only surviving colonial remains

Filthy Corner

The area now known as Pointe aux Canonniers was dubbed by early Dutch settlers De Vuyle Hoek (Filthy Corner) because so many of their ships were swept on to the reef.

are a 19th-century light-house and a few cannon in the grounds.

GRAND BAIE

The appeal of **Grand Baie** ❹, billed as the island's premier resort, lies in the profusion of shops, restaurants and cafés not attached to hotels strung around a turquoise bay dotted with pleasure craft. Called overrated by some islanders, who point to its lack of pavements, congested coast road, tatty tourist shops and night-time prostitution, Grand Baie for most European holidaymak-

A tropical idyll at Grand Baie

ers is heaven, thanks to its slow, easy-going atmosphere and range of hotels, apartments and self-catering accommodation mostly within walking distance of the action. In Chemin Vingt-Pieds, **La Croisette** (www.gblc.ennovatek.com), a massive entertainment and leisure complex with shops, restaurants, cinemas and luxury apartments, is set to be Mauritius's premier shopping destination.

Centre of operations is Sunset Boulevard where designer shops rub shoulders with cafés, souvenir shops and the Sportfisher Big Game Fishing Centre. Tour operators line the street, offering car and bicycle hire, excursions and trips to offshore islands, plus all water-based activities, such as diving, water skiing, windsurfing, parasailing, underwater safaris and undersea walks. For a swim, avoid the beach on the coast road and head to **La Cuvette** at the north of the bay. It has a parking area, showers, food kiosks and toilets, and you can swim beyond the basalt rocks on the right-hand side and onto the beach fronting the celebrity-starred Royal Palm Hotel.

NORTH FROM GRAND BAIE

Just 2km (1 mile) north of Grand Baie is **Péreybère**, which offers affordable self-catering apartments, a fairly buzzing nightlife in bars and beach-fronted eateries, safe swimming and a handy bus route linking it with Port Louis. It is popular with independent travellers as an alternative to brash Grand Baie. At weekends, convoys of mobile food wagons, ice-cream vans and lorries crowded with picnicking families from Port Louis liven up this normally quiet beach.

Shallow bays and rocky coves combine to make a picturesque 6km (4-mile) journey north via Bain Boeuf to the island's most northerly point, **Cap Malheureux**. A pretty red-roofed church surrounded by grassy lawns overlooks the lagoon to the wedge-shaped island of Coin de Mire, directly opposite. In 1810 a massive British naval force anchored off its shores before marching to Port Louis to take possession of Mauritius.

Looking out over Coin de Mire

More sparkling beaches backed by casuarina forests unfold at Anse la Raie, before the road hits the cane fields leading to **Grand Gaube**, a fishing hamlet fanned by northeast trade winds. Beyond the gates of the area's two hotels, Legends and Paul and Virginie, lie a pleasant public beach, children's play area and coast road with colourful tumbledown village stores.

South of Grand Gaube is the bustling town of **Goodlands** where a textiles and clothing market (Tuesday and Friday) attracts hundreds of locals and tourists. Directly opposite the market is the island's biggest maker of model ships, **Historic Marine** (Mon–Fri 9am–5pm, Sat–Sun 9am–noon; tel: 230 283

9404; www.historic-marine.com; free guided tour), where models based on original museum plans, and nautical furniture, are produced and sold.

To the southeast of Goodlands is **Poudre d'Or**, where an obelisk on the headland opposite the reef commemorates the sinking of the *St Geran* in 1744 and the drowning of a young engaged couple. The event inspired 18th-century writer, Bernadin de St Pierre, to pen the romantic Mauritian classic, *Paul et Virginie*, after whom a hotel at Grand Gaube is named. Some of the wreckage from the *St Geran* is displayed at Mahébourg's National History Museum (see page 50). For a great day's snorkelling in translucent waters, local fishermen will ferry you to uninhabited **Île d'Ambre**. For some bracing walks along windy, deserted rock-studded beaches, head further south to isolated **Roches Noires**, but do not swim here because the currents are dangerous.

NORTHERN OFFSHORE ISLANDS

Operators in Grand Baie offer full-day tours with barbecue lunch to all the offshore islands, including Île aux Cerfs (see page 47) in the east and Île aux Benitiers (see page 65) in the west. Most popular for swimming and snorkelling are the reef-enclosed waters between **Flat Island** and **Gabriel Island**. On Flat Island, pathways, a lighthouse and cemetery bear testimony to those who died during the 1856 cholera epidemic, while the deserted beaches of Gabriel have changed little since the island's days as a quarantine post. Great views of the coast from the open sea make a cruise to **Coin de Mire** a wonderful day out, although going ashore here is not possible due to the island's crumbling volcanic rock. **Round Island** (which isn't round) is home to the rare Telfair skink and **Serpent Island** (which has no snakes) is a bird sanctuary. Both are designated nature reserves for which you need permission to enter.

PAMPLEMOUSSES AND THE SUGAR MUSEUM

The north's top attraction is the **Sir Seewoosagur Ramgoolam Botanic Garden** ❺ (daily 8.30am–5.30pm; charge), formerly called the Royal Botanic Gardens, at **Pamplemousses**. Well signposted on the motorway north of Port Louis, the gardens are only a 30-minute drive from Grand Baie. A visit makes a pleasant change from the coast. Official guides (charge) may offer to show you around the 25-hectare (62-acre) site, or you can wander at will. Mazes of shady palm-lined avenues border indigenous Mascarene island flora. Impressive sights include the graceful yellow and white lotus flowers of the Lotus Pond; and the huge, flan-case-shaped leaves of the giant Amazon water lilies in the Lily Pond. Other specimens include the curiously named marmalade box, chewing gum and sausage trees. In 1735, under Labourdonnais, the area was used as a market garden, which provided fresh supplies for the ships calling at Port Louis.

Giant Amazon water lilies in the botanic gardens

Among the other notable sights here are the white wrought-iron gates, which were included as an exhibit at the Great Exhibition of 1851 at London's Crystal Palace. The imposing **Chateau de Mon Plaisir**, built in the mid-19th century by the British, was named after

Mill wheels at L'Aventure du sucre Museum

the original chateau occupied by Pierre Poivre, the French Intendant and horticulturist who first introduced many of the species that grow here today. Opposite the gardens, is the 18th-century **Church Saint François d'Assises**, fringed by a handful of restaurants, cafés and souvenir shops.

L'Aventure du Sucre Museum (daily 9am–5pm; charge; tel: 230 243 7900; www.aventuredusucre.com), just 0.5km (0.25 mile) from Pamplemousses at Beau Plan Sugar Estate, is a former sugar factory converted into a fascinating museum. You can easily spend half a day here exploring, with the aid of videos and interactive displays, the history of sugar and its importance to the social and economic development of Mauritius. Original equipment includes huge mill wheels, evaporation tanks and an old sugar boat authentically anchored in a reconstructed indoor harbour. Guided tours are also available as well as free sugar tastings. There is a shop selling speciality sugars and unusual souvenirs, plus the pleasant Fangourin restaurant.

THE EAST

Some of the island's most luxurious hotels are located on the east coast, but this area remains essentially isolated and rural, an area of agricultural land, broken by vistas of picturesque mountains, slow-moving fishing villages and inviting beaches. Many hotels lie in sheltered positions, protected from the southeast trade winds that blow year round but are especially strong from May to November. Away from the beaches, there are some rewarding historic and scenic attractions to be explored. Getting around by public transport can be frustrating and it may be better to hire a car.

BELLE MARE TO ÎLE AUX CERFS

The main town is **Centre de Flacq**. There's not much to see here apart from the Sunday market, tumbledown shops and a 19th-century courthouse, but there are plenty of buses and taxis to other parts of the island. East of the town through flat cane fields is beautiful **Belle Mare ❻** public beach lapped by an idyllic lagoon. Barbecue areas, the odd mobile food wagon and meandering paths through the casuarinas replace the straw parasols and swanky sophistication of the hotels flanking the beach, while old kilns testify to the former industry of coral *Belle Mare beach*

burning. There are several golf courses in the area.

South along the coast road, the small village of **Trou d'Eau Douce** has narrow streets, colourful tourist shops and simple restaurants. Tour operators provide a 10-minute ferry service from here to **Île aux Cerfs ❼**. The island consists of 280 hectares (700 acres) of luxuriant woodland, an 18-hole golf course, two eateries and a few souvenir shops. You can wander along shaded paths, find deserted beaches, snorkel and swim, go parasailing, enjoy a barbecue lunch at uninhabited Île Mangenie or take a speed-boat trip to Mauritius's longest river, the boulder-strewn Grande Rivière Sud-Est, which terminates in cascading waterfalls at Beau Champ.

Heading south from Beau Champ, fields of sugar cane stretch towards the Bambous Mountains, which form a dramatic backdrop to the isolated fishing villages of Deux Frères, Quatre Soeurs and Grand Sable. The road hugs the shore until rising to **Pointe du Diable** (Devil's Point), a grassy headland, where Creole superstition credits the devil with upsetting the compasses of passing ships. Two cannon dating back to 1759 mark the site of a French battery, from whose ruined walls there are fine views of **Île aux Phares**. This was the island on which the Dutch imprisoned Rodrigues' first settler, François Leguat (see pages 73 and 75), in 1693.

Vieux Grand Port, lying in the shadow of Lion Mountain, marks the beginning of an historic route along the coast. In 1598 the Dutch landed here, called it Warwyck Bay and built Fort Frederick Henry at the north of the town. It is now a collection of ruined walls with evidence of 18th-century French defences. The adjacent **Fort Frederick Henry Museum** (Mon, Tue, Thur–Fri 9am–4pm Sat 9am–noon; free; tel: 230 634 4319) contains a model of the original fort, artefacts unearthed during a 1997 archaeological dig, and audio-visual displays of the history of the Dutch East India Company in Mauritius.

At **Ferney**, to the west of Vieux Grand Port, you can take a guided nature walk from the Visitors Centre to the Ferney Valley Forest and Wildlife Reserve (daily 9am–5pm; charge; tel: 230 729 1080; www.valleedeferney.com). This 200-hectare

Beach at Île aux Cerfs

(500-acre) reserve contains endemic flora and fauna and viewpoints. Further north at **Domaine de l'Etoile** (daily 9am–5pm; charge; tel: 230 729 1050; www.cieletnature.com) some 2,000 hectares (4,900 acres) of rolling landscapes of streams and valleys offer ideal conditions for quad biking, trekking, archery and jeep safaris.

MAHÉBOURG TO BLUE BAY

Lying on the southern shores of the bay of Vieux Grand Port with views of Lion Mountain to the north is **Mahébourg** ❽, named after Mahé de Labourdonnais. It is a laid-back village, which in spite of its bustling Monday market and dilapidated stores and shops, strives to maintain its colonial heritage: the streets, laid out in a grid pattern, are named after early European settlers; a **waterfront obelisk** facing the pretty islet of **Mouchoir Rouge** commemorates the Battle of Grand Port in 1810; an 18th-century washhouse called **Le Lavoir**, off Rue de la Passe, is still used as an outdoor laundry; and there's a quirky **boat-shaped monument** to Ferney-born journalist Remy Ollier, who represented the interests of the black population in the mid-19th century.

A short stroll north of the village is **Cavendish Bridge**, which crosses La Chaux River to **Ville Noire**, named after black slaves who arrived in appalling conditions to work the French-owned sugar plantations. Tucked around the back streets is the oldest factory in Mauritius, the **Rault Biscuit Factory** (Mon–Fri 9–11am, 1–3pm; charge; tel: 230 631 9559), where *biscuits manioc* are made from the cassava root. This family-run firm offers guided tours finishing with vanilla-flavoured tea and freshly baked biscuits. A scenic drive past the factory along the B7 through cane fields backed by the gorgeous Creole Mountains leads to **Riche en Eau**, where chimneys mark the site of early family-run sugar estates.

Mahébourg's **National History Museum** (Mon, Wed–Fri 9am–4pm, Sat–Sun and public holidays 9am–noon; free; tel: 230 631 9329) is housed in a renovated colonial mansion on the A10 leading out of the village towards the airport. Built in 1722 and the former residence of a French dignitary, it was hastily turned into a makeshift hospital in 1810 where injured commanders of the French and British fleets convalesced following the three-day Battle of Grand Port (see page 20).

The museum contains maps and documents from the Dutch, French and British colonial periods, a frieze of the Grand Port Battle, portraits of maritime personalities, wooden palanquins used by slaves to transport their masters, and artefacts recovered from East India Company shipwrecks. The most prized exhibits are the bell from the doomed *St Geran*, sunk off the east coast in 1744, and Labourdonnais' four-poster bed.

North of Mahébourg at Anse Jonchée is **Kestrel Valley** ❾ (daily 8.30am–4.30pm; charge; tel: 230 634 5011). This

300-hectare (750-acre) reserve offers deer and wild boar hunting and trekking along steep walking trails through forests of spice plants and native trees. The area is renowned for sightings of the Mauritius kestrel. You can lunch at Le Panoramour restaurant and enjoy panoramic views of the reefs and islets of Vieux Grand Port, and stay overnight in one of the several simple bungalows. In the foothills is **Domaine de Ylang Ylang**, an old distillery where ylang ylang plants are cultivated for their aromatic, essential oils.

A Mauritius kestrel

Southeast of Mahébourg is the nature reserve of **Île aux Aigrettes** ❿ (Mon–Sat 9.30am, 10am, 10.30am, 1.30pm, 2pm, 2.30pm, Sun mornings only; charge; tel: 230 631 2396; www.mauritian-wildlife.org), opposite Preskil Beach Resort. The Mauritian Wildlife Foundation (MWF) created the reserve to protect native flora and fauna, so a trip here will appeal to the conservation-conscious rather than those wanting a water-based fun day out. Be advised that the island gets very hot (take a hat and water) and can accommodate only 20 visitors at a time on tours, which are led by knowledgeable MWF guides. You will see giant Aldabra tortoises and bands of the once-endangered pink pigeon, rare plants and paths bounded by bronze models of extinct fauna. During World War II the island was used for military purposes. The old generator room from that time has been renovated and includes a rooftop platform, which affords sweeping views of a canopy of indigenous trees that represent a microcosm of Mauritius's original coastal habitat. A shop and small museum display models and paintings of many extinct species.

Back on the mainland via the high-walled seaside bungalows of Pointe d'Esny the road ends at **Blue Bay ⓫**, where an idyllic beach backed by casuarina trees faces the private islet of Île des Deux Cocos. The area lies in a designated marine park, whose crystal-clear waters make for excellent snorkelling and diving.

THE SOUTH

The remote, wild south, with its undulating cane-clothed landscapes, forests, waterfalls, rivers and mountains, has none of the bustle of the more popular tourist resorts of the north. Its appeal lies in its natural beauty and a feeling that you are going

Black River Gorges National Park

back in time. However, the west part of the south coast has undergone a transformation with the completion of smooth, wide roads that give access to hotels and inland attractions.

The southern beaches are narrower than elsewhere and rivers flowing from the uplands have prevented coral reefs from forming in many places. In the southwest corner of the island are the last of Mauritius's indigenous forests. By contrast, the southeast is a flatter, sugar-producing region of small towns and villages linked by roads crossing streams and rivers.

Whether you drive yourself or join a guided tour there are several ways of exploring the south: from Curepipe in the centre of the island, combining it with a trip to the Black River Gorges; from Bel Ombre in the west where several luxurious hotels herald the start of an easy route east along the south coast; or from Mahébourg in the southeast.

BLACK RIVER GORGES NATIONAL PARK

Runaway slaves or *marrons* used to hide in the rugged mountains, gorges and forests that today make up the **Black River Gorges National Park ⑫,** an area of 6,575 hectares (16,250 acres) in the southwest. Elsewhere, little remains of the island's indigenous flora and fauna, but here you might spot the Mauritius kestrel and the green echo parakeet – two birds recently brought back from the brink of extinction – the white tropic bird, the cuckoo shrike and bands of macaque monkeys.

Many tourists combine a shopping trip to Curepipe with a scenic drive through the national park, heading southwest to La Marie and passing cool pine forests to the island's largest reservoir, **Mare aux Vacoas**. Continue for 7km (4 miles) to the crossroads called **Le Petrin**, where an information centre (tel: 230 258 0058) marks the entrance to the park. Here you can buy a map of the walking trails, have a picnic in the adjacent Le Petrin Native Garden or explore the boardwalk leading over

Festival lake

During the annual Maha Shiv-aratree festival at Grand Bassin, thousands of devotees make offerings to the goddess Shiva and pray at the waterside Hindu temples. At other times of the year, the lake is a place of quiet contemplation broken only by the sound of birdsong and cheeky chattering monkeys.

marshy heathland, where native flora and medicinal plants are being regenerated.

A diversion 2km (1 mile) east of Le Petrin on the B88 takes you to the water-filled volcanic crater of **Grand Bassin** watched over by a tower-ing sculpture of the Hindu god Shri Mangal Mahadev. It is the island's tallest statue at 32m (108ft). Hindus call the lake Ganga Talao ('Ganges Lake') as they believe that the waters are linked to the River Ganges in India.

Heading into the national park itself, drive south of Le Petrin via **Plaine Champagne**, an isolated plateau of privet choked with the invasive Chinese guava, whose fruit islanders gather for its vitamin C content in winter. On the way, keep an eye out for the *bois de pomme* and *bois de natte* trees, often draped with orchids, ferns and lichens, so characteristic of the island's upland forest. Further west are two viewpoints over the Black River Gorges. The first is **Alexandra Falls**, but the more spectacular views are from the **Black River Gorges Viewpoint**, 8km (5.5 miles) from Le Petrin, where the deep, dark gorges unfold. The peaks of Rempart Mountain and Corps de Garde form a backdrop in the northwest.

The road twists and turns steeply downhill to **Chamarel** where coffee is grown on the slopes. This tiny village, with its church, village hall and string of simple restaurants, attracts tour groups heading to the **waterfalls**, the highest in Mauritius at 83m (272ft). Best seen after heavy rains, the falls tumble from the River St Denis in the Black River Mountains to form the River du Cap.

Nearby are the **Coloured Earths** (daily 6am–6pm; charge; tel: 230 483 8298), a unique landscape of multi-coloured earth, thought to have been the result of uneven cooling of molten rock. Facilities include a cafeteria, shop and viewing platforms.

A tortuous but picturesque route from the Coloured Earths to Baie du Cap on the south coast cuts through sugar-cane fields and thick plantations of banana and travellers palms. At Baie du Cap turn left to join the B9 to Bel Ombre or right to reach Le Morne.

BEL OMBRE TO SOUILLAC

The area of **Bel Ombre** is associated with philanthropist and planter Charles Telfair, who arrived in Mauritius from Ireland in 1816. He bought the Bel Ombre Sugar Factory and turned it into a 'model sugar estate' by treating his slaves humanely, upsetting the local slave-owning fraternity by doing so. The factory and banana plantations that once fringed the coast are now given over to tourism.

Chamarel Waterfalls

Sugar is still grown in the area and transported to nearby factories, but all that remains of Telfair's factory are the chimney and outbuildings.

Now occupying the site are the Telfair Hotel, an 18-hole golf course, and the elegant 19th-century **Château de Bel**

Ombre, a former haven for visiting estate dignitaries that has been transformed into an upmarket restaurant. The Telfair, the Heritage and other neighbouring hotels can arrange excursions into the nearby private **Domaine de Bel Ombre** (tel: 230 623 5522; www.domainedebelombre.mu), where there are great walking trails and quad- and mountain-biking opportunities. Steep, winding tracks lead to **Frederica**, where a ruined mill stands on the site of an old sugar factory. Further inland, **Val Riche Forest**, with its deer-hunting area and miradors, is home to many indigenous trees.

West of Bel Ombre is the small fishing village of **Baie du Cap**, followed by the magical deep inlet of the same name. Chug along the old concrete parapet across the bay, the Savanne Mountains forming a natural backdrop; this area has been earmarked for tourism development.

If you continue west along the coast road, you reach Mauritius's most famous landmark and a symbol of slavery, **Le Morne Brabant** ⓭. Inscribed on Unesco's World Heritage List, this forebidding mountain towering over the hammerhead-shaped peninsula, now fringed with beach hotels, marks the former hideout of many runaway slaves. When slavery was abolished in 1835, a posse was sent here to announce the news. Fearing that they would be hunted down, the slaves flung themselves into the waters below rather than surrender.

East of Bel Ombre, the coast road speeds past cane fields, crossing bridges over the jungley banks of the **River Jacotet**. The river flows into **Baie de Jacotet** opposite Ilot Sancho, where British and French troops clashed in 1810. There are rumours of buried pirates' treasure here.

The smooth B9 coast road from **Pointe aux Roches** to Riambel provides access to the luxurious Shanti Maurice Hotel and public beaches. Your hotel can organise a visit to the 2,400-hectare (6,000-acre) **Domaine du Cerf D'Or** (tel: 230

697 7941/230 422 3117) at **St Felix Sugar Estate** at **Chamouny**, which includes a mountain lodge, spice garden, nature trail and restaurant. You can also drive inland from Chamouny to **Bassin Blanc**, where a precarious parking area allows views into a water-filled crater where the rare green echo parakeet and the Mauritius kestrel thrive in the surrounding forest. Further east, the sea off Pomponette is known for its treacherous currents, but there is safe swimming at SSR Public Beach just before the peaceful hamlet of Riambel.

There's nothing to detain you at Surinam, but it's worth stopping at **Souillac** ⓮, 2km (1 mile) further east, to explore a handful of nearby attractions. In the 19th century, steam ships laden with cane from nearby estates would shunt along the coast to Port Louis from the **old port**, on the banks of the River Savanne where a 200-year-old sugar warehouse has been converted into Le Batelage restaurant.

Le Morne Brabant

Just 5km (3 miles) inland from the old port, a bumpy ride through cane fields leads past the chimney of an early 19th-century sugar factory and the colourful Mariamen Temple before reaching the 10m (33ft) high **Rochester Falls**. The waters spill over from the Savanne River and years of erosion have shaped the basalt rock into upright columns. After heavy rains, young islanders use this place as an outdoor pool.

Just opposite Souillac's bus station is **Telfair Gardens**, perched on the edge of a cliff and shaded by Indian almond trees and banyans. To the west is the **Marine Cemetery**, which contains some of the island's oldest tombs, including those of Mauritian historian Baron d'Unienville (1766–1831) and poet and writer Robert Edward Hart (1891–1954), who lived in the village.

COLONIAL HOMES

St Aubin is a fine example of a once widespread style of colonial architecture. Traditionally constructed from wood, colonial houses were kept cool by spacious and airy verandas at the front and rear, and by windows decorated with ornate wooden friezes or lambrequins. Wooden shutters could be closed during cyclone periods.

Unless maintained against the ravages of tropical conditions, wooden houses deteriorate very quickly and, sadly, many colonial houses have been allowed to fall into ruin. However, there are some superb privately owned residences hidden in the sugar estates and also in the back streets of Port Louis. The finest example is the 1859-built Château Labourdonnais (daily 9am–5pm; charge; tel: 230 266 9533; www.chateaulabourdonnais.com) at Mapou. Restored to its former glory in 2010 this residence contains original furniture and an ambience of yesteryear. You can dine in colonial splendour in the restaurant surrounded by magnificent lawned gardens or stroll through the estate and tropical orchards.

A 10-minute stroll east of Telfair Gardens is the **Robert Edward Hart Museum** (Mon, Wed–Fri 9am–4pm, Sat 9am–noon; free; tel: 230 625 6101), Hart's former home. This prolific Franco-Irish poet wrote works in French and English from this charming coral-built bungalow, which he called **La Nef** (The Nave).

Le Gris Gris

The interior contains personal belongings, laid out much as he would have left them.

For views of a savagely wild coast from a grassy windswept headland, walk a few minutes east to **Le Gris Gris**, the most southerly point of Mauritius and a place rumoured to be associated with black magic. Some fine cliff walks reveal ghostly silhouettes of black rocks bashed by ferocious seas, including La Roche qui Pleure (The Crying Rock), which bears an uncanny resemblance to Hart's profile.

On the A9, 5km (3 miles) northeast of Souillac, is the grand 19th-century colonial residence of **St Aubin ⑮** (Mon–Sat 9am–5pm; free; www.saintaubin.mu), set in spacious flower-bordered lawns dotted with trees and with an anthurium plantation. You can have tea on the veranda if the place isn't heaving with tour groups, or order lunch (reservations essential; tel: 230 626 1513). Tea is grown in the highlands around Bois Cheri 10km (6 miles) north. You can see how tea is processed and packaged at the **Bois Cheri Tea Museum and Factory** (Mon–Fri 8.30am–4pm, Sat 8.30am–2.30pm; charge; tel: 230 507 0216). A guided Tea Route Tour, which can be booked through tour operators, starts at Domaine des Aubineaux, a former tea planter's residence at Curepipe,

Giant tortoise and friend in La Vanille reserve de Mascareigne

and is followed by a visit to the factory, tea tasting at a hilltop pavilion and lunch at St Aubin.

At **Rivière des Anguilles**, also off the A9 and just after the river of the same name, is **La Vanille Reserve de Mascareigne** ⑯ (daily 8.30am–5pm; charge; tel: 230 626 2503; www.lavanille-reserve.com). Allow a couple of hours to visit this nature reserve, and douse yourself with insect repellent before exploring the shaded walking trails. You'll see thousands of commercially farmed Nile crocodiles in secure enclosures, luminous green geckos, chameleons, insects, butterflies and giant tortoises. A shop sells crocodile products and the restaurant specialises in crocodile meat dishes. Further north is the **Britannia Sugar Factory**, surrounded by spacious lawns and pineapple plantations. Like many other factories in Mauritius, it is no longer engaged in sugar production.

There's not much of interest on the B8, which heads east towards the airport at Plaine Magnien, other than a diversion to Le Souffleur, a blow hole in the cliff at L'Escalier midway along the coast. At one time during high tide, powerful waves would send spouts of water into the air. After years of erosion, the spout these days is more a cloud of spray.

THE WEST

The island's 50km (30-mile) long west coast, rapidly rising in popularity among overseas visitors, is dominated by the mountains and forests of the Black River area and fringed by white beaches and turquoise lagoons. The climate is hotter and drier than that of other parts of Mauritius. The seas off the Black River coast are a mecca for big-game fishermen, especially between September and March when warm waters attract giant marlin and tuna. Added to these attractions are fantastic sunsets, great inland nature walks, fabulous dive spots and easy access to Port Louis.

SOUTH FROM PORT LOUIS

Just off the A3 south from Port Louis and almost mid-way down the west coast is the popular resort of **Flic en Flac**. There is a concentration of restaurants, shops, supermarkets and Mediterranean-style apartment complexes, but the saving grace is the long white beach backed by casuarinas, a lagoon and distant views of Le Morne Brabant in the south. By contrast, **Wolmar**, less than 2km (1 mile) to the south, is quieter and dominated by half a dozen stylish beach-fronted hotels. All along the coast the diving is excellent, with several wrecks to explore, including *Kei Sei 113* and *Tug 11*, sunk deliberately in the 1980s to form artificial reefs (see page 85).

The area north of the A3 cuts through the sugar-cane plantations of **Medine Sugar Estate**, which owns much of the land

JEWISH DETAINEES

In the grey-walled St Martin's Cemetery, 127 identical tombstones are a reminder of events that took place during World War II. In 1940, British authorities refused 1,580 Eastern European Jewish refugees entry to Palestine. Regarded as 'illegal immigrants', they were shipped to Mauritius and detained in refugee camps at Beau Bassin Prison. They remained there until the end of the war. Families still return to Mauritius to visit the graves of those who died in the camps.

around Wolmar as well as the residential area of Albion. It is also one of the most successfully diversified estates on the west coast, with interests in tourism, golf resorts and real estate. During the cane-cutting season, tour operators may organise a guided tour of the factory, which also includes a distillery where you can buy local rum.

A few kilometres beyond the entrance to the sugar estate is the busy little village of **Bambous**. Tucked into cane fields to the north is **St Martin's Cemetery**, where you can see the graves of Jewish detainees who died in captivity at nearby Beau Bassin Prison during World War II (see box).

Quad biking in Casela Nature and Leisure Park

Casela Nature and Leisure Park ⑰ (Mon–Fri 8am–5pm, Sat–Sun 8am–4.30pm; charge; tel: 230 452 2828; www.caselapark.com), on the A3 south from Bambous, makes a break from the beach and a fun day out. You could easily spend a whole day at the 10-hectare (25-acre) park, which sits on the flanks of Rempart Mountain. As well as some 1,500 birds, including the rare Mauritius kestrel and pink pigeon, housed in 90 aviaries, there are giant Aldabra tortoises, tigers, lemurs, antelopes and zebras. The top attraction is the chance to walk with lions and cheetahs in the wild, accompanied by their handlers. Children can pet farm animals, and there's a fine restaurant with rolling views of cane-clothed countryside. The more adventurous can join photo safaris, go quad- and mountain-biking or join exciting nature escapades in the adjacent Yemen Estate, where Java deer roam in a savannah landscape reminiscent of Africa. You are likely to spot wild boar, giant fruit bats and mongoose.

TAMARIN

Tamarin ⑱, 6km (4 miles) south, famous for its salt-making industry, is named after the tamarind trees, introduced by the Dutch, that are a feature of the area, especially in the undulating terrain of the Tamarina Golf Estate. Luxury villas and an 18-hole golf course make Tamarin a fashionable place to holiday. The stylish Riverland Sports and Leisure Complex, with a large pool and cafeteria, attracts a trendy crowd; the long-established Tamarin Hotel stages regular jazz nights, and the bay attracts dolphins and body surfers. Meanwhile, the village retains a timeless atmosphere, its seaside bungalows and cheap pensions fringing a tranquil bay where the coral reef is subdued by waters flowing from the Rempart and Tamarin rivers in the central highlands. At sunset there are magnificent views of Rempart Mountain, resembling a mini-Matterhorn in a tropical setting.

The **Martello Tower Museum** (Tue–Sat 9.30am–5pm, Sun 9.30am–1pm; charge; tel: 230 471 0178), at **La Preneuse**, sits on the northern side of the Grande Rivière Noire Bay, 2km (1 mile) south of Tamarin. It is the best-preserved Martello tower in Mauritius and has walls that are 3.5m (11ft) thick. A visit takes you past cannon and the paraphernalia needed to fire them, including cannon balls; you'll see the fascinating engineering of the tower, how rain was collected in underground reservoirs and how gunpowder was kept dry. The British built this and

Martello towers

Martello towers were defensive forts built by the British in various coastal locations in Britain and the empire during the Napoleonic Wars. Their round shape and thick walls gave them great resistance to cannon fire.

four other towers on the large bays of the west coast to protect against enemy invasion at a time when there was much rivalry between the French-speaking population and the British authorities over the intended emancipation of slaves. Two other towers survive – at La Harmonie, to the south of the Grande Rivière Noire Bay, and at Pointe aux Sables, just outside Port Louis.

Still on the A3 south, the next village, **Grande Rivière Noire**, is the west coast's game-fishing centre. Off the coast, and beyond the reef, the seabed drops abruptly to a depth of nearly 600m (2,000ft), the habitat of several big-game species. Just before the village, opposite the Pavillion de Jade restaurant, a road cuts through sugar cane for 5km (3 miles) to the northern entrance of the Black River Gorges National Park. You can only drive as far as the visitors centre (daily 9am–5pm), where you can collect maps and information. Serious hikers may enjoy an uphill 10km (6-mile) trek along the strenuous Macchabée Trail, crossing rivers and streams, to a spectacular forest viewpoint. The other way to get into the park by car is to drive south to **Grande Case Noyale** and turn inland to Chamarel.

Grande Rivière Noire village sits on the estuary of a river that flows through some of the most rugged areas on the island. Once the poorest region of Mauritius, with a predominantly Afro-Creole population, the area is showing signs of prosperity, although life still trundles on at a leisurely pace. A gated complex of hillside villas and the gleaming shopping and restaurant complex of Ruisseau Creole contrast sharply with the brightly painted stores, simple eateries and weathered timber-built colonial **post office** and **police station** of the village further on. Next to the post office is the **cemetery**, where the founder of the Mauritius Turf Club, Colonel Edward Draper, is buried.

At Grande Case Noyale, the cream-coloured church of Mater Dolorosa lies at the foot of a steep road marking the turn-off for the 5km (3-mile) drive to Chamarel. The road was originally built in 1812 to give access to the remote uplands and, although it is well surfaced, there are numerous hair-pin bends. Spectacular views of the west coast unfold as you climb the timbered foothills of the Black River Mountains, and you may spot bands of macaque monkeys on the way. Two restaurants, La Crete and Varangue-sur-Morne, perched in the hills, provide panoramic views of the countryside, coast and clam-shaped **Île aux Benitiers** nestling in the lagoon. Both establishments are good pit stops before pressing on for the Coloured Earths and Waterfalls.

Grande Rivière Noire

Rose Hill church

THE PLATEAU TOWNS

The towns of the plateau have merged into one unattractive urban sprawl to form the district of Plaine Wilhems in the centre of the island. Some 30 percent of the island's population live in this busy, and often traffic-choked region. In spite of these negatives, the towns are worth visiting for an insight into local lifestyles, the climate is cooler than elsewhere and there are isolated pockets of architectural interest.

The towns were formed a little more than 100 years ago as a result of several migrations from Port Louis after fire, disease and cyclones sent inhabitants scurrying to the healthier uplands. Today the area of Plaine Wilhems contains the towns of Rose Hill–Beau Bassin, Quatre Bornes, Vacoas–Phoenix and Curepipe.

Many tour operators offer shopping trips to the towns, often combining them with a drive into the Black River Gorges, but you can just as easily drive yourself by taking the marked exits anywhere along the motorway which links Mahébourg in the south with Grand Baie in the north.

ROSE HILL–BEAU BASSIN

The Royal Road links the towns of **Rose Hill** and **Beau Bassin**, which are effectively one, with a combined population of about 111,000. Rose Hill's centrepiece is the Victorian-built **post office**, a former railway station, standing proud amid the chaos of the bus station fringed by ubiquitous food stalls and shopping arcades. The town is showing signs of modernity, new roads leading east past weather-beaten buildings to the Cyber City complex at Ebene. Here, **Cyber Towers I and II**, occupied by foreign companies, are symbols of 21st-century development and reflect the island's desire to become a leader of information technology in the Indian Ocean region.

Meanwhile **Arab Town**, in Royal Road, Rose Hill's main shopping street, is a reminder of the immediate present. Here, you can barter for just about anything under the sun among an untidy collection of corrugated-iron covered stalls. Nearby, tumbledown shops are packed with incongruous displays of everything from statues of Hindu gods and the Virgin Mary to cosmetics and car parts. Further south is the colonial-style **Town Hall**, dating back to 1927 and a fine example of Creole architecture, and the Max Boullé Art Gallery, which sometimes exhibits works by local artists.

Beau Bassin, to the north along the Royal Road, is less frenetic than Rose Hill and has a couple of sights worth visiting. **Balfour Gardens** (daily 10am–6pm), in Swami Sivananda Street, has great views of the Moka Mountains across a ravine to a waterfall, which tumbles into the Grande Rivière North West. Next door is **Le Thabor**, a Catholic church pastoral centre. Charles Darwin stayed here in 1836, leading him to remark, 'How pleasant it would be to pass one's life in such quiet abodes'. More ravine views unfold in this tranquil area, dubbed 'The English Quarter' during colonial times when British diplomats and the aristocracy lived here.

At **Moka**, about 4km (2 miles) east of Rose Hill, is the modern university complex, the massive shopping Mall of Mauritius at Bagatelle and **Le Réduit**, the president's official residence (twice a year; check with the tourist office for dates). The French built this magnificent chateau in 1748 on a peninsula isolated by two ravines as a country residence and retreat for the wives and children of the French East India Company in the event of an invasion. It later became the residence of the British governor.

Nearby, the Mahatma Gandhi Institute has the **Folk Museum of Indian Immigration** (Mon–Fri 9am–3.30pm; free), which traces the 19th-century migration of Indian cane workers to Mauritius.

QUATRE BORNES

Many people speed through **Quatre Bornes** after a shopping trip to the European-style shopping mall at **Trianon**, unaware that there are some lovely colonial houses tucked away in the back streets. La Foire market, on Wednesday and Saturday in

INVITATION TO A BALL

Le Réduit was the setting for a piece of philatelic history in 1847. In that year, the Mauritian colonial authorities introduced postage stamps, one with a value of one penny, the other of two pennies. Britain had issued the first stamp only seven years before. The story goes that a local engraver was told to produce the stamps quickly so that some of them could be used by the governor's wife, Lady Gomm, to send invitations to a ball at the residence. The stamps, bearing the head of Queen Victoria, were mistakenly printed with 'Post Office' instead of 'Post Paid'. The mistake has made the few surviving examples very highly valued by collectors.

the heart of town, has good buys in clothing, household goods, and fruit and vegetables, and there are reasonable shops and eateries in the main Grand Route St Jean. To the west is the distinctive **Corps de Garde Mountain** at 720m (2,326ft), which runaway slaves used as a lookout post. Rising up the flanks of the mountain are Hindu

Moka mountain peaks

temples where Tamil devotees celebrate the annual Cavadee Festival. To the south is the hump-shaped **Candos Hill**.

VACOAS–PHOENIX

Vacoas was a former British land-based communications base, HMS *Mauritius*, whose old colonial-style buildings are now the headquarters of the paramilitary Special Mobile Force. The chaos of the bus station and market, so characteristic of many Mauritian towns, is mitigated by more tranquil scenes: glimpses of rural England, with quiet, shaded avenues, an 18-hole golf course at the private Gymkhana Club and the stone-built **St Columba's Church**, where services are held monthly in English.

Phoenix is home to a brewery producing the local beer, as well as food-manufacturing companies and the sprawling Jumbo and Les Halles shopping complexes.

Nearby, the **Mauritius Glass Gallery** (Mon–Sat 9am–5pm; free; tel: 230 696 3360) includes a small museum featuring exhibits by various conservation groups, such as the Mauritian Wildlife Foundation and Friends of the Environment. In the workshop you can watch highly-skilled glass-blowers, who use recycled glass, and buy unusual products in the adjacent showroom.

CUREPIPE

Curepipe , the highest plateau town at 550m (1,840ft), is situated halfway between Mahébourg and Port Louis. In the 18th century, soldiers and travellers would rest and 'cure' or clean their pipes, hence the name. It was the first plateau town to be settled, mainly by the Franco-Mauritian population in the 1860s, who spilled into the suburbs of Floreal and Forest Side, where their descendants still live in grand colonial houses hidden by high bamboo hedges.

Invariably cloud-capped and rainy, the town is not particularly inspiring, but a shopping expedition can turn up some good buys: porcelain and silk in the Chinese shops in Royal Road; designer goods, home decor and fashion accessories at Galerie des Îles, **Currimjee Arcades**, also in Royal Road; and sophisticated knitwear at Floreal Square where the **Textile Museum** traces the development of the

French-style architecture in Curepipe

textile industry with the aid of interactive displays.

At Forest Side, next door to the **Comajora Model Boat Factory** in La Brasserie Road, is the privately run **Boat Museum** (Mon–Fri 8am–5pm; free; tel: 230 675 1644). It's worth visiting for its collec-

Botanical Gardens

To the west of Curepipe are the 2-hectare (5-acre) Botanical Gardens in Botanical Gardens Street. Its avenues, bounded by lakes, lawns and indigenous plants, are perfect for a quiet stroll.

tion of over 100 model boats. The museum's owner is passionate about sailing history and is happy to share his knowledge with visitors. Curepipe is also a popular gateway to the Black River Gorges.

Curepipe's most attractive buildings are sandwiched between Elizabeth II Avenue and Ste-Thérèse Street near the market, whose concrete chimneys rise like foghorns against an often grey sky. Here the 1920s-built **Carnegie Library** and the impressive Creole-style architecture of the **Town Hall** contrast with the modern Lake Point complex, with its shops and casino. The complex overlooks gardens containing a bronze statue of Paul and Virginie, star-crossed lovers of the *St Geran* shipwreck and the central characters in Bernadin de St Pierre's romantic 18th-century novel.

Also worth visiting is **Trou aux Cerfs**, a 15-minute walk or short taxi ride (vehicular access between 8am and 4pm) from the centre of town. This 300m (980ft) diameter crater was formed as a result of volcanic activity millions of years ago and is now choked with silt, water and a dense forest of vegetation. At 650m (2,100ft) above sea level you could be on the roof of paradise were it not for the urban sprawl of the plateau towns below, but the views of the mountains, especially on a clear day, are truly spectacular.

Returning to shore on Rodrigues

RODRIGUES

The island of Rodrigues, a semi-autonomous region of Mauritius since 2002, lies 560km (350 miles) east of Mauritius. Shaped like a fish, it is 18km (11 miles) long and 8km (5 miles) wide, making it the smallest of the Mascarene trio. Only a few navigable channels penetrate the fringing coral reef, which protects a lagoon almost twice the island's size. Running the length of Rodrigues is a hilly ridge, from which a series of steep valleys drop to a narrow coastline. Even though the flight from Mauritius takes only 90 minutes, you can't help feeling quarantined from the rest of the world when you bump along the runway at Sir Gaëtan Duval Airport at Plaine Corail in the south. If you have time, you can go to Rodrigues by ship (see page 124).

About 41,000 people live here. The island's distinct Creole-African atmosphere is in complete contrast to Indian-dominated Mauritius. Also unlike Mauritius, the island is a relative newcomer to tourism. With stunning coves and bays, deserted beaches, a shallow islet-dotted lagoon, great diving, snorkelling, hilly walking trails, duty-free shopping, and a friendly, courteous people, Rodrigues makes a simple, unpretentious and at times quirky holiday destination.

PORT MATHURIN

Port Mathurin ⑳, the pint-sized capital, is home to some 6,000 people. It sits snugly on the north coast and was probably named after a French settler, Mathurin Morlaix, who arrived in 1726. Under the French, slaves from Mozambique and Madagascar, and settlers from Mauritius, increased the population to just over 100 in 1804. Nobody took much notice of Rodrigues until the British launched an attack from its shores before taking Mauritius in 1810. They restructured Port Mathurin and laid out the present town in grid style, naming many streets after surveyors and civil servants. Rodrigues's regional authority have now renamed the British-influenced street names with those of a French flavour.

A good place to start your exploration is from the boat-shaped jetty on the waterfront where a **memorial** stands to volunteers who fought in World Wars I and II.

The Saturday **market** in Wolphart Harmensen Street attracts early risers as islanders set up stalls of fruit and vegetables at 6am. You can find souvenirs such as baskets and wallets made from woven vacoas leaves, as well as bottles of chillies, home-made chutneys, and fruit and vegetables. The market sells out quickly, and by 10am everybody has packed up and gone home.

FRANÇOIS LEGUAT

François Leguat led the first group of settlers on Rodrigues in 1691, and left behind a fascinating record of his time there, *Voyages and Adventures*. In it, he describes the island's unique flora and fauna, the latter including a species of giant tortoise weighing over 135kg (300lb). There were so many tortoises that the beaches were covered in them, and Leguat used the shells as stepping stones to reach the sea (the species later became extinct). The book was so accurate that 19th-century naturalists and geologists used it as an early text-book. Leguat's name would have been forgotten had it not been for Rodrigues' star attraction being named after him (see page 80).

View over Port Mathurin

The main artery of the town is Rue de la Solidarité one block back from the waterfront, where shops, no more than corrugated iron shacks with handwritten nameplates nailed to the door, contrast with a rash of duty-free shops in Rue François Leguat and Rue Morrison. In Rue Max Lucchesi you can find unusual handicrafts, such as snazzy briefcases, straw hats and fiery home-bottled chillies. At the western end of Rue de la Solidarité is the tiny, white six-minareted **Noor-ud-Deen Mosque**. The island's only mosque, it was built in 1912 for the first Muslim settlers, who had arrived in 1907 as textile merchants.

Still in Rue de la Solidarité, hidden by white walls and fronted by a cannon, is the last vestige of British colonialism, the 1873 **Island Secretary's Residence**. It now houses the tourist office (Mon–Fri 9am–4pm; tel: 230 832 0276). The wide veranda is shaded by an Indian almond tree beneath which visiting colonial experts would discuss the next big move in island affairs;

A short stroll east leads to the Anglican **St Barnabas Church**, shaded by gardens and trees. Originally designed by an Eastern Telegraph cableman in 1903 as a shingle-roofed wooden chapel, it's been modernised and enlarged to encompass the Rodrigues College. Most Rodriguans are Catholics and the little **Saint Coeur de Marie Church** in Ricard Street sees a regular Sunday congregation. The daubing of foreheads with ashes in the sign of the cross on Ash Wednesday, and processions on Easter Day, are serious traditions.

Over the **Winston Churchill Bridge**, which crosses the River Cascade, is the location of the first settlement on the island, in 1691, by French Huguenots fleeing religious persecution.

Led by François Leguat (see page 73), they lived for the next two years on 'very wholesome and luxurious foods which never caused the least sickness', as Leguat wrote, and feasted on fruit and palm wine, before returning to Mauritius only to be imprisoned by the Dutch on Île aux Phares as spies.

Further upriver towards **Fond La Digue** is Port Mathurin's only hotel, the delightful Creole-style Escale Vacances, set in a wooded valley overlooking the river. You can have some adventurous uphill walks along a jungley boulder-strewn track to Mont Lubin, where at dusk the Rodrigues fruit bat comes out to feed on jamrosa trees.

For some unique island handicrafts, visit the **Careco Workshop** (Mon–Fri 8am–3pm, Sat 8am–noon) at Camp du Roi at the back of town. It is a charity where coconut craft and jewellery items are made by disabled people. An apiary also produces the clear and distinctly flavoured Rodriguan honey, which has consistently won international awards.

Visitors wanting some nightlife, meanwhile, should look out for hand-written bills advertising *une grande soiree dansante*. These are big nights out, not to be missed, when you can let your hair down. On pay days and holidays or roughly once a

Port-Mathurin's tourism offiice in an old colonial building

month, everyone from babes in arms to robust Rodriguan grannies dance to seggae and reggae beneath flashing lights, surrounded by smooching couples. Try the alfresco discos at Les Cocotiers at Camp du Roi or the Recif at Anse aux Anglais.

AROUND PORT MATHURIN

A short stroll to the east of Port Mathurin is **Anse aux Anglais** ㉑ (English Bay) where in 1761 a British fleet arrived and stayed for six months. Like the French ships that came before them, the Royal Navy's vessels transported thousands of giant tortoises – valued for their meat – from here to neighbouring Réunion. By the end of the 18th century, the Rodrigues tortoise, which originally may have numbered around 200,000, had become extinct.

In 1901 cablemen from the Eastern Telegraph Company (later Cable & Wireless) laid a submarine telegraph cable linking the island with Mauritius, thus completing the line of communication between Australia and Europe. The cablemen lived in quarters at nearby **Pointe Venus** where the manager's colonial-style residence, which later saw service as the island's first hotel, has re-opened as a comfortable four-star billet. There are good views across Port Mathurin from the headland where astronomers recorded the Transit of Venus in 1761, 1874 and 2004.

At low tide, near the Pointe Venus Hotel, groups of fisherwomen, known as *piqueuses ourites*, make their living spearing octopus, which they hang out to dry in the sun. A stiff uphill climb from Anse aux Anglais via the tranquil beachside bungalows of **Caverne Provert** leads to a headland where there are resplendent views over sandy-bottomed **Grand Baie**, just 4km (2 miles) east of Port Mathurin. It's a lovely spot with only a church and makeshift football pitch. From Grand Baie the road peters out to become a narrow uphill track that leads towards the sweeping deserted beach at **Baladirou**. A less strenuous way of getting there is to take a 40-minute boat ride along the coast from Port Mathurin.

Just 2km (1 mile) to the west of Port Mathurin is **Baie aux Huitres** (Oyster Bay), an enormous bay surrounded by hills and deep forests of casuarinas. Many civil servants posted from Mauritius live here with their families, along with the predominantly European descendants of the first French settlers. For the best views, drive up to **Allée Tamarin**, a hamlet at the back of the bay.

INLAND FROM PORT MATHURIN

The bus station to the west of Port Mathurin has plenty of buses to take you on a bone-shaking journey around fearsome hairpin bends to the spine of the island, where little villages overlook the north and south lagoons. Buses stop at around 4pm, so leave plenty of time to return.

At **Pointe Canon** there are panoramic views of the

School visit

At Camp du Roi, next to the Careco Workshop, is the Gonzague Pierre-Louis Special Learning Centre (Mon–Fri 8am–2pm), a school for sight- and hearing-impaired children. Pupils are pleased to receive visitors and the teachers are happy to give you a tour.

Drying an octopus catch,
Anse aux Anglais

capital. On this windswept headland you'll find a British cannon juxtaposed with a white statue of the Virgin Mary, **La Reine de Rodrigues**. On 1 May, the approach road and hills are a riot of colour with islanders trekking towards the statue to celebrate Labour Day. On 15 August, large numbers attend outdoor mass here to celebrate Assumption Day. The road climbs to **Solitude**, where a forest bounded by deep valleys and eucalyptus trees is the habitat of colonies of fruit bats.

Mont Lubin, a busy little village of tumbledown shops, gives the impression of being at the top of the island, but the highest point is actually **Mont Limon** at 398m (1,289ft), a five-minute walk east. Many tourists pass this way to visit **Grande Montagne Nature Reserve** (tel: 230 832 5737) for its walking trails and small museum, before continuing to Pointe Coton and the isolated eastern beaches.

Rodrigues' biggest place of worship, the twin-towered Gothic-style Cathedral of Sacre-Coeur, is west along the Mont Lubin road at **Saint Gabriel @**. Islanders built the cathedral in 1939, using donkeys to carry sand from the coast, and their own labour to bring cement, lime, blocks of coral, corrugated iron and timber up the narrow mountain paths. It seats 2,000 people and Sunday morning mass is a colourful event.

The 5km (3-mile) stretch of road between the hamlets of **Petit Gabriel**, **Quatre Vents** and **Mangues** is peppered with glimpses of translucent blue lagoons bordered by a thin pencil-line of ivory-white foam marking the reef.

You have to pass through **La Ferme**, a large noisy village, where Pope John Paul II held mass during his 1989 visit, to reach **Cascade Pistache**, 2km (1 mile) west of the village. This crater, hewn out of granite, is surrounded by grassy hills; the waterfall tumbling into Rivière Pistache looks particularly beautiful after heavy rains. As an alternative, take the road northwards to **Baie du Nord** for a scenic 9km (5-mile) coastal drive back to Port Mathurin, passing isolated homesteads swathed in poinsettias and hibiscus, and causeways filled with mangroves at **Baie Malgache**.

THE SOUTH

From Mont Lubin, in the centre of the island, it is only a 6km (31/2-mile) journey to **Port Sud-Est**. The road snakes its way down hillsides, twisting and turning along a series of hair-pin bends, each giving glorious vistas of Port Sud-Est, where small coral atolls dot the lagoon. Your journey's end is the **Morouk Hotel**, sitting in an isolated clifftop location. The

ÎLE COCOS

For a day that will stay in your memory long after the holiday snaps have been stashed away, don't miss Île Cocos, 4km (2 miles) west of Rodrigues. Here you'll have nothing to do but pad barefoot along floury white beaches beside a gin-clear lagoon while listening to the chatter of birds. This island, one of 18 inside Rodrigues lagoon, was transformed into a nature reserve in 1980 after studies revealed that out of an estimated 12 species of indigenous birds only two were left. It is now the last refuge of the fody and the brush warbler. Tour operators will arrange the necessary permits for a visit. The boat ride to Île Cocos ends 1km (0.6 mile) from shore because of shallow water; you walk the rest of the way.

Brown noddies on Île Cocos

nearest village to here is **Songes**, where boxy cyclone-proof houses are scattered along the hillsides. Attractions include leisurely walks to the pretty beach of **Petit Gravier** along the coast, and picnic and snorkelling excursions to Hermitage and Cat islands.

A visit to the coral caves for fascinating stalactites and stalagmites in the southwest corner of the island at **Caverne Patate** ㉓ some 18m (60ft) below the ground, is not for the faint-hearted. In 1786 bones believed to be those of the dodo were found but later searches in 1894 proved that they belonged to a relative of the dodo, the solitaire, the bird described by François Leguat in 1691.

Safer well-lit caves along timber walkways and handrails can be explored with qualified guides at the **François Leguat Giant Tortoise and Cave Reserve** ㉔ (daily 9am–5pm; charge; www.tortoisecavereserve-rodrigues.com) at nearby **Anse Quitor**. Here a conservation programme to restore the island's natural habitat is paying off with the planting of thousands of endemic plants and a colony of over 500 introduced Giant Aldabra tortoises at various stages of development. Allow half a day for a guided walk which includes the island's only museum devoted to history, fauna and flora.

THE EAST

The **Cotton Bay Hotel**, at Pointe Coton in the east, was the first three-star hotel to open in Rodrigues and is popular with walkers and beach lovers. It is flanked by low coral cliffs and overlooks the best swimming beach of the island. From here you can walk to **Roche Bon Dieu**, a phallus-shaped rock symbol protruding from the earth and said to be a gift from God. There are more superb beaches, accessed by pathways on coral-topped cliffs, to **Anse Ally**, **Saint François** and **Baie de l'Est** and to the protected forest land at **Tasman**. Due east from here the nearest landfall is the western coast of Australia, some 5,500km (3,410 miles) away.

The forested area is fenced off to stop cattle grazing, but the watchman will let you in to experience some wonderful walks. Paths bounded by great forests of casuarina trees and acacias lead to a plateau of dead coral, where massive white rollers pound the reef, in some places less than 100m (300ft) from the shore. From here the paths rise and dip into the lovely coves and bays of **Grand Anse**, **Trou d'Argent** and **Anse Bouteille** before linking up to Port Sud-Est.

Cascade Pistache

WHAT TO DO

SPORTS

Mauritius's greatest attraction is, of course, the sea. The coastal waters, with few exceptions, offer safe swimming in shallow blue lagoons. Most hotels offer free water-based activities, which include snorkelling, windsurfing, water-ski-ing, sailing in hobie cats, use of pedalos, and trips in glass-bottom boats. Scuba diving, big-game fishing and parasailing are also popular and can be booked through hotels or inde-pendent tour operators. Similar facilities are available in Rodrigues, but since that island's lagoon is shallow there are no motorised water sports or parasailing and big-game fish-ing is relatively new.

The seabed and coral reefs are the habitat of myriad col-ourful fish and other marine creatures. Several operators offer enticing excursions, such as dolphin-watching cruises, underwater safaris, cruising to offshore islands, sky-diving and helicopter tours, which give magnificent views of the lagoons and coastline.

Recent years have seen a proliferation of green tour-ism ventures, for which res-ervations are essential. The undulating landscapes are ideal for horse-riding, quad-biking, four-wheel drive 'soft' safaris, mountain-bik-ing, cycling and canyoning. Golfing on scenic courses, tennis, walking and hiking are also very popular.

Sail away

For a trip back in time, try a cruise on the 150-year-old *Isla Mauritia*, which you can book through your hotel or direct through Yacht Charters (tel: 230 263 8395). This magnifi-cent sailing ship, with a crew in turn-of-the-19th-century uni-forms, sails from Grand Baie and drops anchor at Baie du Tombeau for a barbecue lunch and a snorkelling session.

Windsurfing over warm waters

WATER ACTIVITIES

Big-game fishing. Mauritius holds the world record for big marlin and hosts the annual Marlin World Cup competition in November at the Centre de Pêche, Grand Rivière Noire, in the southwest. The best time for big-game fishing is between October and the end of March or April, when the waters beyond the reef teem with powerful blue and black marlin, yellow-fin tuna, wahoo, sailfish, bonito and various species of shark. The larger hotels have their own boats, and a number of private companies offer fishing excursions, such as the **Corsaire Club** (tel: 230 265 5209), **JP Charters** (tel: 230 5729 0901, www.blackriver-mauritius.com) and **Sportfisher** (tel: 230 263 8358, www.sportfisher.com) at Grand Baie. A one-day fishing trip for a maximum of four people is about R 40,000 and includes drinks in a fully equipped boat with experienced crew. In Rodrigues contact **Rod Fishing Club** (tel: 230 875 0616, www.rodfishingclub.com).

The seabed and coral reef

Sailing. Cruising in cata-marans or yachts along the coast or to visit offshore islands is immensely popular. Many charter companies offer full- or half-day excursions that include lunch, drinks and snorkelling equipment. One of the best is **Land and Sea Adventures** (tel: 230 261 1724) at Pointe aux Piments, which offers an exhilarating day out to Gabriel Island.

Clear blue waters at Île aux Cerfs

In Rodrigues you can sail to several deserted islands within the lagoon through **Rod-tours** (tel: 230 831 2249).

Scuba diving. Dozens of dive centres, all affiliated to CMAS (World Underwater Federation), PADI (Professional Association of Diving Instructors) and BSAC (British Sub Aqua Club), are attached to hotels and offer courses for beginners and the more experienced. All adhere to strict international-ally safety regulations and provide multi-lingual instructors, together with all the necessary equipment.

Beginners start off in the hotel pool before taking the plunge into the lagoon. Veteran divers should head for the long-established dive centre based at Villa Caroline at Flic en Flac, which offers specialist and night diving.

Some of the best dive sites are off the west coast at Flic en Flac where there are several wrecks to explore, including the *Kei Sei 113* and *Tug 11*, sunk deliberately in the 1980s to form artificial reefs and now home to giant moray eels and myriad reef fish. Popular dives in the

Rock-climbing

north include the wreck of *The Silver Star*, from 1992, and between two offshore islands, Gabriel and Flat. In the east, the prevailing winds limit diving opportunities, but some interesting dives can be made in and around the passes through the reef. The best place to dive on the south coast is at the Blue Bay Marine Park where a sheltered lagoon and several sites beyond the reef will reward you with spectacular views of underwater life. On Rodrigues there are dive centres at the Cotton Bay Hotel (tel: 230 831 8001) and Mourouk Ebony Hotel (tel: 230 832 3351).

Snorkelling. Many visitors are content to spend their entire holiday snorkelling in the safety of the lagoon and over the shallow reefs. If you're staying in a hotel, all equipment is provided; if you're not, there's no shortage of shops selling masks, fins and goggles. You can also buy waterproof laminated cards from bookshops, which identify some 40 common species of reef fish. Even if spending a short time snorkelling, do wear a T-shirt and douse yourself in high-factor sun cream to avoid sunburn.

Submarine safaris. For an hour-long trip in a submarine that explores some interesting shipwrecks, contact **Blue Safari Submarine** (tel: 230 265 7272, www.blue-safari.com). *Le Nessee*, bookable through tour operators in Grand Baie, is a semi-submersible vessel with particularly good viewing chambers that enable you to have eyeball-to-eyeball contact with many marine species. Both the Blue Safari Submarine and *Le Nessee* leave from Grand Baie.

Undersea walks. A boat takes you from the shore to a platform inside the lagoon and, wearing your swimsuit, you are equipped with a helmet, which supplies fresh air piped from the surface by oil-free compressors. You are then gently lowered from the platform to the seabed where you can stroll amid wonderful coral gardens and even feed the fish by hand. The helmet allows verbal communication with an experienced diver, who gives you a guided tour of the lagoon. This activity is perfectly safe for children over seven, and will also appeal to non-swimmers. Undersea walks can be booked through **Captain Nemo's Undersea Walks** (tel: 230 263 7819) at Grand Baie or **Aquaventure** (tel: 230 415 5040, www.underseawalkmauritius.com) at Belle Mare.

Horse-riding on the beach

An idyllic place for golf

LAND-BASED ACTIVITIES

Adventure Tourism. Mauritius is just starting to tap its potential for adventurous activities. Extreme sports enthusiasts can go canyoning and rock-climbing with **Vertical World** (tel: 230 697 5430, www.verticalworldltd.com), which also has great hiking opportunities. **Casela Leisure and Nature Park** (tel: 230452 2828, www.caselapark.com) offers similar activities, as well as photo safaris. For hunting and trekking contact: **Kestrel Valley** (tel: 230 634 5011); for quad and mountain-biking and trail walking contact **L'Etoile** (tel: 230 433 1010, www.cieletnature.com); or **Yemaya** (tel: 230 752 0046, www.yemayaadventures.com) **Mautourco** (tel: 230 670 4301, www.mautourco.com) has several four-wheel drive 'soft' safari options into the hinterland to see hidden landscapes and indigenous wildlife. In the **Black River Gorges National Park** (tel: 230 464 4016), starting from Le Petrin or from the Black River Visitors Centre in the lower gorges, there are some 60km (37 miles) of easy to strenuous walking trails through tropical native forests. When choosing an operator for an adventurous activity, consider our health and medical-care information (see page 125), and check your travel insurance to make sure you're covered in case of an accident.

Horse-riding. A number of stables take visitors on rides through breathtaking hills and countryside, including **Vieille Cheminee** (tel: 230 483 4249/725 5546) at Chamarel, which has five gentle horses; **Domaine les Pailles** (tel: 230 286 4225), just outside Port Louis; and **Horse Riding Delights** (tel: 230 265 6159) at Mon Choisy Leisure Park. Rides start from R2,100 per adult and R1,900 for children under the age of 15. The Maritim Hotel, on the northwest coast, also has private stables for the use of guests. Reservations for horse-riding are essential.

Hunting. Deer and wild-boar hunting are traditional Mauritian pastimes, and are becoming popular with some visitors. Contact Kestrel Valley (as above) or Domaine des 7 Valleés (tel: 230 631 3336, www.domainedes7vallees) to find out how to arrange a hunting party that includes accommodation in rustic bungalows. The hunting season for deer is from June to September. Wildboar hunting is a year-round activity.

Racing at the Champs de Mars, Port Louis

Cycling. The flat coastal regions make for some easy rides. Bikes can be booked through your hotel, and there are plenty of operators in the resorts who rent bikes by the hour, half day or full day.

Golf. There are nine-hole courses at St Geran (tel: 230 401 1688), Shandrani (tel: 230 603 4343), Maritim (tel: 230 204 1000) and Sofitel (tel: 230 453 8700). There are 18-hole courses at Anahita (tel: 230 402 2200), Belle Mare Plage (tel: 230 402 2600), Tamarina (tel: 230 401 3006), Paradis (tel: 230 401 5050), Bel Ombre (tel: 230 623 5522) and at Île aux Cerfs (tel: 230 402 7720) on the east coast. Equipment, clubs and caddies can be hired. All hotels have a clubhouse with a locker room and shop. Pros can also be hired for lessons. Non-guests have to pay an entry charge. There is also a private 18-hole course at the Gymkhana Club at Vacoas.

TYING THE KNOT IN PARADISE

Couples seeking the perfect location for their wedding are finding it in increasing numbers among the romantic seascapes and luxury hotels of Mauritius. But before vows can be exchanged, there are some legal necessities to attend to.

To get married on Mauritius, a couple must have a minimum of 24 hours' residency for civil ceremonies and 15 days' residency for religious ceremonies. They must have a valid 10-year passport and bring original birth certificates, decree absolute if divorced and, if getting married within 10 months of the divorce, proof that the bride is not pregnant. Those aged under 18 must have parental consent. If names have been changed by deed poll, legal proof of the change needs to be provided. Once in Mauritius the couple attend the Registrar's Office to sign an affidavit that they are both free to marry. For further information contact the Registrar of Civil Status, 7th floor, Emmanuel Anquetil Building, Port Louis, tel: 230 201 3203. UK tour operators specialising in weddings are Elite Vacations (www.Just2Mauritius.com) and Kuoni (www.kuoni.co.uk).

The sega, a traditional dance imported by African slaves

OTHER ACTIVITIES

Horse racing. The season begins in May and culminates in November with the Maiden Cup, the grandest and most important race of the year. Races are held every Saturday afternoon and some Sundays at Champs de Mars in Port Louis. For further information contact the **Mauritius Turf Club** (tel: 230 212 2212, www.mauritiusturfclub.com).

Helicopter tours. Air Mauritius helicopters (tel: 230 603 3754, www.airmauritius.com/helicopter.htm) offer sightseeing tours and splendid photographic opportunities of the coast and the interior. A 15-minute trip costs R32,000 per helicopter, which can seat four people.

Spas. The large hotels have luxurious spas where health and beauty packages include everything from reiki and reflexology to stone therapy and shiatsu. For the ultimate in personal pampering, try any of the following hotels: Residence (tel: 230 401 8888); Telfair (tel: 230 601 5500); and Heritage (tel: 230 601 1500). For dedicated ayurvedic treatment try the Surya Ayurvedic Spa Centre (tel: 230 263 1637), at Pereybere.

Skydiving. For the jump of a lifetime go tandem skydiving for spectacular countryside and seascapes from 10,000ft with Skydive Mauritius (tel: 230 5499 5551, www.skydivemauritius. com). Prices from R11,500 per person.

NIGHTLIFE AND ENTERTAINMENT

Most nightlife in Mauritius takes place in the hotels, which stage themed after-dinner shows often featuring the *sega*, a traditional dance imported by African slaves. Sexy and sensual, it is performed by voluptuous hip-wiggling women and accompanied by musicians beating wildly on the *ravan* (a goatskin tambour), the *maravan* (a hollow tube filled with dried seeds) and the triangle. Rodriguans have their own form of *sega* and traditional music, which you can see at hotels and a three-day Festival Kreol, which takes place at the end of October.

Away from the resorts, nightlife is low-key, apart from several bars and discotheques in Grand Baie, Flic en Flac and Tamarin. Cultural activities are usually poorly advertised, so it can be hard to pin down what's going on. Shows and musicals, invariably in French or Creole, are often performed at Mahatma Ghandi Institute at Moka, the Swami Vivekananda Conference Centre at Pailles and the Institut Français de Maurice at Rose Hill. Casinos de Maurice (www.casinosofmauritius.com) manage four casinos at Curepipe, Domaine les Pailles, The Caudan and Flic en Flac. The Senator Club (www.senatorclub-mu.com) also has casinos at Port

Model ships

Model ships of interest to collectors may be purchased from First Fleet Productions (tel: 230 698 0161) at Floreal, and Historic Marine (tel: 230 283 9404) at Goodlands.

Louis, Triolet, Grand Baie, Mahébourg and Flac. All the island's cinemas screen English-language films dubbed into French.

SHOPPING

Local handicrafts include embroidery, paintings, basketware, model ships, pottery, recycled glassware and toiletries made from locally produced essential oils. Since the closure of many textile factories and increased competition from Asia, jewellery, knitwear and textiles are not the bargains one might expect. Many tour

Hand-carved sailing ship model

operators organise shopping trips to Port Louis, Floreal and Curepipe, or you can take a taxi and do it yourself. Shops to look out for are: **Adamas** (tel: 230 686 5246), **Passion** (tel: 230 263 4384) and **Cledor** (tel: 230 698 8959), for diamond and precious stones set in fabulous designs; **Etoile d'Orient** (tel: 230 210 4660), for duty-free antiques, silks, carpets and jewellery; and **Floreal Square** (tel: 230 698 7959), for cashmere and knitted goods. Beachwear and designer clothing under the Harris Wilson, Karl Kaiser, Marina Rinaldi and Max Mara labels are also excellent value.

Shops tend to have fixed prices, but you can test your bargaining skills in markets, of which there are dozens throughout the island. The most popular is the **Central Market** at Port Louis, which is renowned for its fresh fruit and vegetables and

Takeaway flowers

Grown on a large scale in Mauritius, anthuriums, with their showy heart-shaped spathes and protruding flower spikes, make distinctive souvenirs or gifts. They are best bought in specially packaged boxes at the airport when you leave.

dozens of stalls selling clothing, spices and souvenirs. **Mall of Mauritius** at Bagatelle and **La Croisette** at Grand Baie, are destined to change retail therapy habits with vast shopping, leisure and entertainment complexes attracting upmarket customers from the more established outlets at Terre Rouge, Phoenix, Grand Baie, Floreal, Tamarin and the characterful arcades and tailor shops at Curepipe.

Supermarkets like **Jumbo** and **Super U** and the delightful **Labourdonnais Farm Shop** at Mapou (tel: 230 266 1533) sell local produce at local prices. Look out for attractive packages containing vanilla-flavoured tea, Chamarel coffee, confectionery and specialty sugars and spices. Green Island rum, liqueurs and punches made from sugar cane also make good souvenirs, along with luggage-friendly vacuum packs of smoked marlin.

In Rodrigues, mind-blowing bottled chillies and pickles, delicious honey and a range of handicrafts made from coconut and other natural materials make unusual souvenirs. They can be bought from **Careco** (tel: 230 831 1766) and other small outlets in Port Mathurin.

CHILDREN'S MAURITIUS

With many safe bathing beaches and professionally run mini-clubs in the larger hotels, Mauritius is a very child-friendly destination. At Domaine les Pailles (tel: 230 286 4225), you can join a horse-drawn carriage tour, visit the mask museum and sugar distillery, and then have lunch at the Dolce Vita restaurant, followed by a dip in the pool.

Animals are always a good bet when the appeal of splashing in seawater and building sandcastles starts to wear thin. Casela Nature and Leisure Park (tel: 230 452 2828) has a zoo and aviary, while crocodiles and tortoises are star attractions at La Vanille Crocodile Park (tel: 230 626 2503). For the very young, try the children's play area on the Caudan Waterfront in Port Louis or the interactive displays at L'Aventure du Sucre Museum (tel: 230 243 79000) at Beau Plan.

Older children with a sense of adventure may like to try their skills and stamina at Parc Aventure, Chamarel (tel: 230 234 5385), where roped ladders and nets festoon trees and rivers, allowing exciting discoveries in a 12-hectare (30-acre) forest. Alternatively they can try quad-biking and archery at Domaine d'Etoile (tel: 230 433 1010, www.cieletnature.com) and, providing they meet height restrictions, go walkabouts with lions and cheetahs at Casela (tel: 230 452 5546, www.safari-adventures-mauritius).

Riding a giant tortoise

CALENDAR OF EVENTS

Many festivals are moveable dates and information on the more unusual events such as fire- and sword-walking, celebrated by the Tamil community, is hard to come by. For more specific information about dates, times and venues of those shown below, contact the tourist office.

January/February *Cavadee* A Tamil festival in which devotees pierce their bodies and faces with skewers as an act of penance to the deity, Muruga. *Chinese Spring Festival* Celebration of the Chinese New Year with firecrackers and displays of dragon dances; the Chinese community offer gifts wrapped in red – symbol of happiness – and there are plenty of celebrations, especially in Port Louis' Chinatown.

February/March *Maha Shivaratree* A celebration by the Hindu community, in honour of Lord Shiva, in which thousands of devotees dressed in white leave their homes in all corners of the island and walk to Grand Bassin, a lake which they believe to be linked to the River Ganges. *Holi A lively*, two-day Hindu festival during which unsuspecting passers-by get squirted with coloured water and powder, which is supposed to bring good luck.

March/April *Ougadi* A low-key New Year festival celebrated by the small minority of Hindu Telegus.

15 August *Assumption Day* Rodrigues's main Christian festival is marked by a huge outdoor mass before the statue of the Virgin Mary at La Reine de Rodrigues, just outside Port Mathurin.

9 September Mauritians of all denominations walk or drive to the tomb of Père Laval at Sainte-Croix, just outside Port Louis, to celebrate the priest's healing powers.

October/November *Divali*, or *the Festival of Light* The Hindu community lights the entire island with small clay lamps and candles, signifying the triumph of good over evil.

Eid ul Fitr Muslims celebrate the end of Ramadam, the month of fasting. The date varies from year to year according to the lunar calendar, and the exact date depends on the sighting of a full moon.

EATING OUT

Food lovers are in for a treat in Mauritius, thanks to a cuisine that's as diverse as the country's people. Wherever you dine you'll find food reflecting influences from India, China, Africa and Europe, from spicy curries and noodles to a melange of exotic fruit and vegetables, sumptuous seafood, and not forgetting the basic burger and chips.

Virtually every restaurant has Indian, Chinese, Creole and European food on its menu and if you don't know what to start with, simply ask for *gadjaks*, which are an assortment of hot snacks such as croquettes, *croustillants* (crispy balls) made from meat, fish, chicken or vegetables, or *gateaux piments* (chilli cakes). Mauritians nibble *Croquettes* throughout the day on *gadjaks* and eat large amounts of rice.

Local beef and lamb is not as tender as the imported cuts from South Africa, Australia and New Zealand, but home-reared chicken and pork is plentiful and good. With the majority of the population being of the Hindu faith, vegetarians are well catered for. Half the fun of eating out is identifying the amazing variety of fruit and vegetables.

You can choose to eat cheaply at roadside stalls,

stick to your hotel, or venture into the resorts and villages where a whole range of restaurants dish up tasty meals at knock-down prices. If you are on an all-inclusive deal, try at least a couple of outside restaurants if only to rub shoulders with the locals and tuck into authentic Mauritian fare. People tend to eat fairly early in the evening, and restaurants are often closed by 10pm.

WHAT TO EAT

INDIAN

Cooks grind herbs and spices to make a *massala*, which is then used with meat, chicken, fish or vegetables to produce delicious curries. Particularly tasty are the *vindaye* curries, made from wine or vinegar and garlic. Some curries are hotter than others, depending on the ingredients used. Plain boiled or saffron-flavoured rice is always served along with chilli sauce. If the curry is too hot, resist the temptation to drink water; instead, mop up the sauce with rice or bread. Indian breads include thick rounds of *roti* (similar to naan), which can be plain or stuffed, or the finer version called *faratha*. A typical Muslim dish is the rice-based *briyani* (biriyani), which is flavoured with a subtle blend of spices and spiked with meat, fish, chicken or vegetables.

Coquelet tandoori

Commonly eaten by all Mauritians, *dhall puri* is an Indian snack that is virtually a meal in itself. Best eaten at the roadside stalls found

Spices play a major role in both Indian and Creole dishes

in resorts, villages and markets because it is freshly made to order, these gut-busting floury pancakes are made with crushed lentils and come stuffed with a tomato, onion and garlic-flavoured sauce called *rougaille*, or any filling you fancy. The luminous green chilli sauce is optional but a smattering gives it that extra bite. *Puris*, on the other hand, are lighter, tiny disc-shaped pancakes, which can be filled with tasty portions of vegetable or meat curry. Try also *gateaux piments* (chilli cakes) and *samoussas* (curry-filled pastries) fresh from the pan.

CHINESE

Chinese dishes are varied and very good value. For something fast and easy, ask for a *mine frite* (fried noodles). If you're feeling adventurous or especially hungry ask for a *mine frite special*, which includes eggs, seafood, chicken or meat. A lighter version that is not unlike vermicelli is *meefoon*. Try also *bol renversee*, an upturned bowl of rice, stabbed with slivers of pork, spicy sausage and chunky chicken, or *fooyang*, an omelette-based offering filled with lobster, crab or prawns. Exotic dishes such as shark-fin soup, sea cucumber and Peking duck are the preserve of upmarket restaurants and should be ordered in advance. Chefs use lots of *ajinomoto* (MSG or monosodium glutamate) to enhance flavour.

CREOLE

Creole food is best described as a fiery fusion of Indian, Chinese and French cuisine; it is traditionally spicy. The end result depends on the whims and imagination of the cook. Culinary wonders emerge from the cooking pot in the form of rich meat and fish *daubes* (casseroles) and *caris* (curries), helped along with the ubiquitous chilli and a cornucopia of herbs and spices. Venison and wild boar are especially good,

An upside-down bowl dish

and plenty of seafood, including octopus and squid, are served in this way, along with a huge variety of local fish, which are usually grilled or fried. Among the exotic vegetables are *coeur de palmist* (palm hearts), known as millionaire's salad; *gros pois* (butter beans); *brèdes* (fresh greens); and *lentilles noires* (black lentils). Pumpkin and

> ### Bounty of the sea
>
> For obvious reasons, fish dishes feature strongly in this island nation's cuisine. Species you may find on the menu include *vieille rouge* (grouper), *carangue* (trevally), *cordonnier* (surgeon fish), *cateaux* (parrot fish), *bourgeois* (red snapper), *capitaine* (white snapper) and *licorne* (unicorn fish).

marrow are also popular. As an accompaniment, you may be offered *achards* or pickled grated vegetables, which are served in small side dishes.

DESSERTS

Desserts in restaurants are usually fresh fruits of the season, ice creams or sweet pancakes, while hotel buffets include a huge variety of European-style sticky pastries, fancy puddings, cakes and cheeses. Summer fruits include mangoes, lychees, water melon and passion fruit, and year round there is plenty of pawpaw, pineapple and banana. Indian sweets are reserved for special occasions, although you can sometimes buy them at patisseries and supermarkets. At Chinese New Year, small, round waxy cakes called *gateaux cirées* are served.

RODRIGUAN SPECIALITIES

The lagoons of Rodrigues provide a natural larder for the islanders, most of whom are fisherfolk. Fish and other seafood are served in hotel and local restaurants in Port Mathurin. Octopus is used in salads, *cari* (curry) and *daube*

Fresh produce is readily available

(casserole), and is less expensive than lobster, prawn and crab, which are simply steamed. Another local speciality is *cono cono*, a mollusc similar to whelk, which is incorporated into a refreshing salad dressed with local limes. Fresh fish is jazzed up and fried Chinese-style with ginger and garlic.

Cari de poulet aux grains (chicken curry with red beans) and *poisson salé* (salt fish) are typical Rodriguan dishes served with plain boiled rice.

Try to go easy on the local *achards* (pickles), however, since they are made from chillies that are considerably stronger than the ones that are grown in Mauritius.

Desserts are not really eaten and fresh fruit is rare, but you can find plenty of shops selling *pain frit* (fried bread sprinkled with sugar), *gateau patate* (sweet potato cake), *gateau manioc* (manioc cake) and *pudding maïs* (maize pudding). All drinks, including beer, soft drinks and water, are imported from Mauritius.

WHERE TO EAT

Most of the luxury hotels tend to be in isolated locations, and dining in local restaurants often involves a taxi ride. Hotel food is plentiful and varied, although often toned down to cater for international tastes. The large hotels often have several restaurants, usually a main buffet-style one and one or more à la carte or beach restaurants. Some hotels have separate facilities for children.

Many local restaurants may seem oddly located, squeezed between, above or behind ramshackle buildings, tucked behind petrol-station forecourts, or hidden deep in the cane fields. The décor may be quirky and the service, although friendly and welcoming, may not always come up to standard. However, the food is fresh and tasty. The more expensive restaurants have air conditioning, tasteful furnishings and pleasant views.

Most top tourist attractions, such as Kestrel Valley, Eureka, l'Aventure du Sucre, and Casela Leisure and Nature Park, have their own restaurants set in gorgeous

LUNCH WITH THE LOCALS

In Rodrigues, unlike Mauritius, it is common for locals to prepare and serve lunch to visitors in their own homes, This concept, known as *table d'hôte*, makes an interesting alternative to restaurant dining and the experience gives a unique insight into local culinary traditions. The food will be typically Rodriguan, such as *cono-cono* (a small whelk), octopus curry, or pork in honey served with pulses on a bed of rice, with fiery pickles and followed by pancakes or papaya sorbet. Details of participating islanders' homes can be obtained from the Rodrigues Tourism Office (tel: 230 832 0866).

Rum treat

If you are invited into a Mauritian home, you may be offered a glass of *rhum arrangé*, a rum-based concoction in which fruits and spices have been left to macerate for months.

locations. These tend to be heavily booked by tour groups, but there is nothing to stop you from making a reservation or, in some cases, just turning up.

Several colonial houses have been restored to their former grandeur and serve a typical Creole lunch of smoked marlin, palm-heart salad, venison or seafood, in stylish surroundings. Try Eureka House at Eureka, Mon Repos at Trianon, Le Jardin de Beau Vallon at Mahébourg, and St Aubin. Reservations are recommended.

There are sophisticated Thai, Japanese and Italian restaurants in the Grand Baie area. Fast-food courts in shopping malls also do a roaring trade in local and international fare. Try the food courts at the Caudan Waterfront in Port Louis, Trianon, Jumbo at Riche Terre, Super U at Grand Baie, and the trendy Ruisseau Creole complex at Tamarin.

DRINKS

Local beers include the Blue Marlin, Stella and Phoenix brands. Rum comes in two varieties, white and dark. The best brand of rum is Green Island, which can be drunk neat or as a cocktail. Cheaper versions to look for are Mainstay Dry Cane Spirit, Goodwill and Old Mill. There are some quite palatable red, white and rosé wines made locally from imported grape concentrate. Labels to look for are Eureka, Chateau Bel Ombre and Saint Nicholas. Australian, New Zealand and South African wines are good value, unlike French wines, champagne and spirits, which are expensive. A good range of potent alcoholic fruit cocktails is also available.

Whisky is also produced locally. Imported blended Scotch whisky is expensive compared with the local King Robert and Findlater brands.

The non-alcoholic drinks include *alouda*. This is made from *agar agar* (boiled china grass) and sugar, soaked *tookmaria* (sweet basil) seeds and flavoured with milk and rose water. You will also find the usual range of soft drinks and bottled mineral water. Milky, vanilla-flavoured tea with plenty of sugar is widely drunk, although black and herbal tea is also available. Coffee comes as *espresso*, filter or *cappuccino*, but in small snack bars and restaurants you are more likely to be served with the instant chicory-flavoured version.

Tropical rum cocktails

Finally, it's wise to drink plenty of water. The ubiquitous 'traveller's tummy', blamed so often on 'dodgy' food, is more likely to be the result of drinking too little water. In Mauritius, especially when it is hot and humid, dehydration is an all too common cause of many stomach complaints, so always carry water with you. Fortunately, it's plentiful and cheap and can be bought in all food shops and petrol stations.

TO HELP YOU ORDER...

Could we have a table? **Je voudrais une table.**
I'd like a/an/some... **Je voudrais...**
The bill, please. **L'addition s'il vous plaît.**

bread **pain**
butter **beurre**
coffee **café**
dessert **dessert**
fish **poisson**
fruit **fruit**
ice cream **glace**
meat **viande**
menu **carte**
milk **lait**

pepper **poivre**
potatoes **pommes de terre**
rice **riz**
salad **salade**
salt **sel**
soup **soupe**
sugar **sucre**
tea **thé**
wine **vin**

Bourgeois – red snapper fish

MENU READER

achards pickled vegetables

agneau lamb

ail garlic

ananas pineapple

bourgeois red snapper fish

brèdes fresh greens

camaron prawns

capitaine white snapper

carangue trevally fish

cari cerf venison curry

cateaux parrot fish

champignons mushrooms

cochon marron wild boar

coeur de palmist palm hearts

cordonnier surgeon fish

crabe crab

daube stewed or casseroled

dessert dessert

entrecote beef rib steak

filet fillet

fruits de mer seafood

gros pois butter beans

haricots beans

jambon ham

kalamar squid

legumes vegetables

lentilles noires black lentils

licorne unicorn fish

marlin fume smoked marlin

melon d'eau watermelon

ourite octopus

petit pois peas

poisson sale salt fish

pommes d'amour tomatoes

poulet/ poisson croustillant crispy fried chicken/fish balls

riz blanc boiled rice

riz saffron saffron-flavoured rice

rougaille tomato, onion and garlic flavoured sauce

sauce piment chilli sauce

saucisse chinoise spicy Chinese sausage

thon tuna

vieille rouge grouper fish

vindaye curry dish based on vinegar or wine and garlic

PLACES TO EAT

We have used the following symbols to give an idea of the cost of a meal for two with soft drinks or beer (imported alcohol can double or even treble the bill). Menu prices do not always include 15 percent VAT, so check first:

$$$$** over R3,000   **$$ R1,000–2,000
$$$** R2,000–3,000   **$ below R1,000

PORT LOUIS

27 St Louis $ *27B St Louis Street, tel: 230 212 5823.* Located in the most interesting part of town, this eaterie offers a variety of both expensive and really cheap options, from Creole cuisine dishes to croissant sandwiches. Open daily for lunch and on Friday for dinner.

Café du Vieux Conseil $$$ *rue du Vieux Conseil, tel: 230 211 0393.* Popular with expats and businessmen, this hideaway café, which is situated across from the Museum of Photography, retains a casual colonial atmosphere in a tree-shaded courtyard carefully concealed from the cacophony of town down a cobblestone alleyway. The service is smart and the menu consists of tasty European and Creole dishes.

Le Courtyard $$$ *corner of St Louis and Chevreau Streets,* tel: 230 *210 0810.* An elegant restaurant that welcomes you in the shade of the terrace just in the heart of the bustling city. This is the place where delightful cuisine and enchanting surroundings become one.

L'Escale $$$$ *Labourdonnaise Waterfront Hotel, tel: 230 202 4000.* This hotel is known as Port Louis's foremost address for world-class, cosmopolitan cuisine. L'Escale serves a fantastic mix of Asian and western dishes in a very friendly and relaxed atmosphere, with view of the Caudan piazza. Open daily.

Dolce Vita $$ *Domaine les Pailles, tel: 230 286 4225.* Enjoy a swim in the open-air pool and then tuck into the large portions of tasty pizza or pasta that are served at this casual Italian restaurant, located just a short drive south along the motorway from Port Louis.

La Flore Mauricienne $$ *10 Intendance Street, tel: 230 212 2200.* La Flore Mauricienne is housed in Port Louis' original meeting place, dating back to the 19th century. This is a perfect pit-stop for a drink or two while people-watching from the terrace. For air-conditioned comfort, try the restaurant where *poisson vindaye* (spicy fish curry) is a local favourite. A good selection of vegetarian options.

Le Jardin $$ *27 Rue St Georges, tel: 230 211 9688.* Tranquil garden location at the back of town noted for delicious Creole cuisine. Ask for the daily lunch special. Free car parking. Closed evenings and weekends.

Lambic $$ *4 Rue St Georges, tel: 230 212 6011.* Mauritius' only gastropub housed in a renovated colonial house attracts a cool city crowd where beers and wine from all over the world and 46 whiskies complement an innovative European and Mauritian menu. Try the Sri Lankan tea with a full English breakfast in the tree-filled courtyard. Wi-fi zone and parking. Open all day until late. Closed Sunday.

Restaurant Canton $ *15 Rue Emanuel Anquetil, tel: 230 242 2164.* This long-established restaurant does a roaring trade at lunchtime. Fast service, eclectic décor and good range of Chinese fare. Open daily. Last orders for evening meals at 7.30pm.

THE NORTH

Café Muller $ *Grand Baie, tel: 230 263 5230.* This charming family-run German coffee shop tucked behind the main coast road is noted for authentic *stollen*, salads and Saturday brunch. Lovely garden setting with tropical atmosphere. Closed evenings.

Cafeteria Pereybere $ *Coast Road, Pereybere, tel: 230 263 8539.* Long-established beach café, perfect for people-watching. Serves excellent Chinese and Creole food, including the local speciality, *poisson gingembre* (fish with ginger).

Café 18 $$ *Powder Mill Road, Pamplemousses, tel: 230 243 7340.* Situated 100m (109 yards) from the gate of the Botanical Gardens, this café offers pleasant décor, friendly service and a good choice of Mauritanian and international dishes, including their locally well-known pastas.

Chez Ram $ *Coast Road, Grand Baie, tel: 230 263 8569*. One of the few restaurants in the area that is always buzzing with tourists and locals. Typical Mauritian cuisine served by the welcoming owner and staff. Closed Wednesday.

La Cigale $ *Royal Road, Pointe aux Canonniers, tel: 230 263 0193*. Tiny restaurant with tables and awnings on the forecourt renowned for delicious home-made pizzas, pastas and meatballs and authentic tiramisu. Closed Monday.

Don Camillo $$ *Grand Baie, tel: 230 263 8540*. Probably the best Italian restaurant in Grand Baie, next door to the Banana Bar. Don't be put off by its location beside the Caltex Petrol Station. Crisp tablecloths, candlelight, excellent service and consistently large portions of seafood, pizza and pasta.

Le Fangourin $$$ *Beau Plan, Pamplemousses, tel: 230 243 7900*. Overlooking lawned gardens, this charming restaurant is well placed as a lunch stop if you are visiting L'Aventure du Sucre Museum. Serves extensive Creole and European fare, and is renowned for delicious desserts using local speciality sugars. Open daily noon–5pm.

Foley's Restaurant $ *7th mile, Triolet, tel: 230 261 4533*. For typical Mauritian cuisine of *briani*, noodles or curry this no-frills restaurant on the main road is renowned for good value and friendly service. Open daily.

Happy Rajah $$ *Royal Road, tel: 230 263 2241*. A hot favourite for authentic South Indian food. Good range of vegetarian and meat dishes, and accommodating staff. Try the selection of naan breads with vegetable *makhanwala*. Decent coffee and Indian desserts served. Handy off-street parking.

La Langouste Grisee $$$ *Royal Road, Grand Baie, tel: 230 263 1035*. A winner of the Fourchette d'Or in 2005 and still recognised as one of Mauritius's best restaurants. Offers very stylish dining from a Franco-Mauritian menu overlooking a beautiful garden. Open for lunch and dinner.

Souvenir Restaurant $ *Coast Road, Trou aux Biches, tel: 230 291 1440*. Across the road from the police station and popular with beachgoers for a casual drink or snack. Sit beneath shaded wooden tables and tuck into chop suey, fried noodles or fish and meat curries. Open daily.

Tante Athalie $$ *Pamplemousses, tel: 230 243 9266*. Named after the family maid who left behind some secret recipes, this quirky little restaurant has vintage cars in the garden and serves genuine home-cooked food only. Try the typical *rougaille*, rice, lentils and *brèdes* (greens). Open for lunch only. Closed Sunday.

Le Tandoor $$$ *Royal Road, Grand Baie, tel: 230 263 1378*. A traditional Indian restaurant which is equipped with a genuine tandoor oven, which gives the food cooked in it an extra-tasty, deep flavour. Open daily.

Wakame $$$ *Royal Road, Pointe aux Canonniers, tel: 230 263 9888*. Authentic Japanese cuisine is served in this modern upmarket restaurant. Watch the chef prepare your goodies in the open kitchen, or help yourself to sushi on the conveyor belt. Try their special prawn tempura roll. One of the better restaurants in the area, popular with expats and worth splashing out for. Closed Tuesday.

THE EAST

La Belle Kréole $$$ *Coast Road Mahébourg, tel: 230 631 5017*. Take a free pirogue ride while experienced chefs prepare traditional dishes such as wild boar, venison and duck à la Creole. Open daily for lunch and dinner.

Chez Manuel $$$ *St Julien Village, Union Flacq, tel: 230 418 3599*. There's a nice buzz and pleasant service in this restaurant, which has lots of dining alcoves in a garden setting. The food is not cheap, but if you're staying on the east coast, dining at Chez Manuel is well worth the taxi fare to get there. Specialities include Chinese and Creole food, grills and seafood. Open for lunch and dinner. Closed Sunday.

Chez Tino's $$ *Royal Road, Trou d' Eau Douce, tel: 230 480 2769.* Serves excellent authentic Creole-Mauritian dishes, fresh seafood and also noodle plates. The house specialty is Mauritian paella. Open daily, Sundays lunch only.

Les Copains d'Abord $$$ *Mahébourg Waterfront, tel: 230 631 9728.* Nautical-themed eatery specialising in Creole and seafood with a sea-facing terrace and splendid views of Lion Mountain. Open daily for lunch and dinner.

Le Jardin de Beau Vallon $$$ *Beau Vallon, Mahébourg, tel: 230 631 2850.* This 100-year-old colonial house was rescued from rack and ruin by the present owners, who have faithfully restored it to its former glory. The shaded dining veranda, wooden floors and antique furniture reflect a bygone era. Surrounded by lush gardens of tropical fruit and trees, it's the place to enjoy Creole specialities such as octopus and green pawpaw curry. Good wine list, excellent service and private parking area. Open daily. Reservations recommended.

Le Kestrel $$$$ *Anse Jonchée, Vieux Grand Port, tel: 230 634 5011.* This rustic restaurant occupies a wonderful spot atop a steep hill on a large hunting estate, giving magnificent views inland towards the hills and over the lagoon to the reefs at Grand Port, where the French and British fought it out in a naval battle in 1810. All produce is sourced from the estate, including the wild boar and venison featured on the menu. Open daily for lunch, but do reserve for dinner.

Symon's $$ *Pointe de Flacq, Belle Mare, tel: 230 415 1135.* It's well worth forgoing your hotel restaurant to come to this pleasant place where you can enjoy local food in a local setting. Seafood, Creole and Chinese food served inside or on the terrace. Closed Sunday.

THE SOUTH

Le Batelage $$ *Souillac, tel: 230 625 6084*. A former warehouse right on the banks of the Savanne River has been converted into an attractive restaurant. The menu offers both European and Creole dishes, and the service is generally unhurried. The laid-back atmosphere changes when tour groups arrive.

Le Chamarel $$$ *La Crete, Chamarel, tel: 230 483 4421*. Rustic-style restaurant offering typical Mauritian cuisine in a gorgeous hillside setting overlooking Île aux Beniters and the lagoons of the southwest. Le Chamarel is a popular lunch stop for tour groups exploring the nearby Chamarel Coloured Earths. Open for lunch noon–3pm. Closed Sunday.

Chateau Bel Ombre $$$$ *Bel Ombre, tel: 230 623 5522*. This magnificent, upmarket restaurant occupies a magnificently restored colonial house in a spectacular setting bordering a golf course. Enjoy an informal lunch of venison or palm-heart salad or opt for a romantic soiree of gourmet dining. Extensive wine list. Serves breakfast, dinner and afternoon tea. Closed Sunday. Reservations recommended.

The Hungry Croc $$ *La Vanille, Reserve des Mascareignes, Riv-ière des Anguilles, tel: 230 626 2503*. Feeling hungry after watch-ing the crocs feed in this nature park? On the menu is an exotic range of Mauritian dishes including crocodile served up in var-ious ways, fritters, curry or kebabs. The less-adventurous can opt for the croc-free croque *monsieur*.

Le St Aubin $$ *Rivière des Anguilles, tel: 230 626 1513*. Step back in time at this handsome 19th-century plantation house on the A9, 5km (3 miles) northeast of Souillac. Enjoy a leisurely lunch of Creole dishes on the open veranda overlooking the lovely gardens. Both house and restaurant are popular with tour groups exploring the tea route. Reservations essential.

Varangue-sur-Morne $$$ *Chamarel, tel: 230 483 5710*. Fabu-lous lunch location overlooking undulating cane fields with views of Beniters Island. Timber stairways lead down to a charming restaurant specialising in Creole and European fare. Ideal if exploring the Black River Gorges. Popular with tour groups, so you should book ahead.

THE WEST

Le Bistrot du Barachois $$ *Route du Barachois, Tamarin, tel: 230 483 7594.* Fashionable hang-out with pleasant outdoor terrace with superb views at the back. Serves European and Creole food, and the menu changes every two weeks. The Lounge next door is a trendy pub-cum-disco. Closed Sunday and Monday.

Domaine Anna $$$$ *Morcellement Anna, Flic en Flac, tel: 230 453 9650.* Upmarket Chinese food in this huge circular restaurant built from local stone. For romantic dining, ask for a private waterside pavilion. Specialities include seafood with palm-heart salad and steamed fish and ginger. Gets busy at the weekend so book ahead. Closed Mondays.

Le Kiosk $ *Ruisseau Creole, Black River, tel: 230 483 7004.* Try the fresh croissants and coffee or grab a *croque monsieur* in this alfresco eatery after a spot of retail therapy in the nearby designer shopping complex. Open till late.

Ocean Restaurant $ *Flic en Flac, tel: 230 453 8627.* Across the road from the public beach, this large Chinese restaurant has an extensive menu. Busy at weekends so best to book ahead. Closed Sundays.

Pavillion de Jade $$ *La Preneuse, tel: 230 483 6151.* This atmospheric Chinese restaurant on a first-floor terrace located opposite the entrance to Black River National Park makes an ideal place to fill up before or after a long walk.

Ze Melting Potes $ *Le Barachois Estate, Tamarin, tel: 230 498 7400.* On the banks of the River Tamarin and part of the modern Riverlands Sports Complex, this trendy location provides all-day snacks and meals beside the pool.

PLATEAU TOWNS

L'Atelier Dumont $$ *1 Cyber City, Ebene, tel: 230 467 2546.* For a special occasion this restaurant excels in Mediterranean cuisine prepared by French chef, Patrice Dumont. Trendy, minimalist and great views of Cyber City. Closed Sunday.

Grain D'Sel Restaurant $$ *Henessy Park Hotel, 65 Ebene Cyber-city, Ebene, tel: 230 403 7200.* A fashionable yet cosy restaurant decorated with black and white photographs taken by local artists. Fresh local produce blends with an array of island and oriental spices. Open daily.

King Dragon $$ *St Jean Road, Quatre Bornes, tel: 230 424 7888.* One of the local favourite restaurants. Owned by the same family as Domaine Anna. The expertly prepared menu boasts Chinese Mauritian cuisine at its finest. King prawns are their specialty. Booking is advised as it is usually full at the weekends.Open daily.

La Potiniere $$ *18 Sir Winston Churchill Street, Curepipe, tel: 230 670 2648.* In the heart of town opposite the Royal College, this cosy restaurant, complete with stone fireplace, sitting area and bar, specialises in game dishes and French and Creole cuisine. Helpful and professional staff.

RODRIGUES

Aux Deux Frères $ *Rue François Leguat, tel: 230 831 0541.* French-run restaurant on first floor terrace specialising in local and French cuisine.

Le Marlin Bleu $$ *Anse aux Anglais, tel: 230 832 0701.* Come here for tasty seafood salads, along with a mix of other seafood, pizza and various local dishes. Open Wednesday to Monday.

Paille en Queue $ *Rue Francois Leguat, Port Mathurin, tel: 230 832 0084.* Popular bolt-hole for Chinese fare and Rodriguan beans, maize, squid and seafood.

A–Z TRAVEL TIPS

A Summary of Practical Information

A

ACCOMMODATION

Hotels in Mauritius are not ranked according to a star-rating system. Nevertheless, many hotels, including the less grand ones, undergo frequent refurbishment and are of a generally high standard with service to match. Don't just turn up and expect to get a room or use the facilities as a non-guest, especially during July, Christmas and New Year, when rooms are pre-booked by overseas tour operators. All beach hotels offer free water-sports, with the exception of big-game fishing and scuba diving, and many have diving schools.

Hotels owned and managed by companies such as Beachcomber (www.beachcomber-hotels.com), Constance (www.constance hotels.com), Naiade (www.naiade-group.hotels-in-Mauritius.eu), Idigo (www.indigohotels.com) and Veranda (www.veranda-resorts. com) are in stunning, often isolated, beach locations.

Increasingly popular with repeat visitors is staying in self-catering accommodation in the main resorts of Grand Baie and Flic en Flac. Generally, the rate you pay depends on distance from the beach and/or your length of stay; the cheapest options are for units some distance from the beach rented for long periods. While these units should be registered with the tourist office, many are not, and you may find that basic safety and security measures don't measure up to Western standards. Always inspect the rooms before committing yourself. Two reputable companies with a wide selection of accommodation are Jet's Villas (www.jet-7.com), Mauritours (www.mauri tours.net) and Elegant Destinations (www.elegantdestinations. co.uk).

Visitors wanting something other than the sun, sea and sand should look for eco-lodges and traditional rural bungalows. Some useful websites to visit include: www.lavieillecheminee.com, www. eureka-house.com, www.relaisdeslodges.com and www.ledomaine delarbreduvoyageur.com.

There are no official camping sites.

> Do you have a single/ double room? **Avez-vous une chambre simple/double?**
> I would like to reserve a room with double bed/ twin beds and bath/shower. **Je voudrais réserver une chambre avec grand lit/deux lits et bain/douche.**
> Is the hotel air conditioned? **Est-ce que l'hôtel est climatisé?**
> Is breakfast included? **Est-ce que le petit déjeuner est compris?**

AIRPORT (see also Getting there)

Sir Seewoosagur Ramgoolam International Airport, locally referred to as SSR (http://aml.mru.aero, tel: 230 603 6000), is at Plaine Magnien near Plaisance, 48km (30 miles) south of the capital, Port Louis. Allow at least one hour to get there by taxi. If you are on a package holiday, your tour rep will meet you and arrange transfer to your hotel. There are no direct buses to the tourist resorts, so independent travellers will have to take a taxi. Agree a fare before accepting a ride, and expect to pay around R1,500 for the journey to Grand Baie.

B

BICYCLE HIRE

Bicycles and helmets in good condition can be rented from the more upmarket hotels. Hotels can also organise guided cycle tours of the island and provide helmets, particularly in the north, which lends itself to some easy rides. Most resorts have bikes for hire, but check brakes, gears and tyres as they are not always in good condition. Punctures can be easily repaired at a tyre repair shop, found in most villages.

BUDGETING FOR YOUR TRIP

Expect to pay handsomely for all those extras if you confine your-self to a hotel. In the real world, basics are remarkably cheap and nearly everything is paid for in Mauritian rupees. Approximately, £1 is worth 55 rupees and US$1 is worth around 35.5 rupees.

Getting there. Despite an open-skies policy, airfares are a major expense, especially if coming from Europe or the US. Package deals through a tour operator can sometimes work out only frac-tionally higher than the airfare.

Accommodation. The sky's the limit at the posh beach-resort ho-tels where you can expect to pay European prices and more. A mid-range hotel costs around R5,000 a night for a double room with breakfast and dinner. Self-catering options are very good value, ranging between R1,000 and R3,000 a day for an apartment or villa.

Meals and drinks. Eating out is cheaper than hotel dining. A simple meal and soft drink or beer will cost less than R400 per person. The cost of meals in the most expensive non-hotel restaurants are similar to European prices. Seafood, excluding lobster, is plentiful and cheap. Imported alcohol and wine can double the bill.

Local transport. Prices for short taxi journeys are on a par with UK prices, although better deals can be struck for half-day (R1,900) or full-day hire (R3,000). Buses are cheap and plentiful, but in resort areas they stop operating after 7pm.

Museums. Apart from government-owned museums there is an entry charge with higher tariffs for non-residents. Expect to pay be-tween R100 and R300 for adults. There are reductions for children.

Watersports. Scuba-diving packages of five and 10 dives are around R6,000 and R10,000 respectively. Experienced divers can expect to pay around R1,800 for a day dive and R2,000 for a night dive. A day on a big-game fishing boat costs around R21,000. It's always worth asking for discounts. Hotel guests can expect free water sports, including windsurfing, snorkelling and water skiing.

					C						

CAR HIRE (see also Driving)

Car hire starts from about R1,500 a day. Rates include insurance, collision damage waiver and discounts depending on length of hire. Credit cards are accepted and you will be asked to sign a blank voucher for the deposit, which will be destroyed in your presence when you return the car. Cars can be collected at the airport or at any pre-arranged point and dropped off when you leave. The more expensive companies are the international ones: Avis (tel: 230 427 6312), Europcar (tel: 230 286 0140) and Hertz (tel: 230 604 3018). Less expensive operators are: Allocar (tel: 230 631 1810) and JR Car Rental (tel: 230 525 10250).

CLIMATE

Mauritius has a tropical maritime climate. There are two seasons, summer and winter. Summer, from November to April, is hot and humid, with short bursts of heavy rain and the occasional cyclone. Winter, from May to October, is pleasant and dry, nights are cooler and there is less humidity than in summer. The southeast trade winds blow all year, keeping the south and east coasts fresher during the summer, but it can get uncomfortably windy at other times. On the coast expect daytime temperatures of 20–25°C (68–77°F) in winter and 25–34°C (77–93°F) in summer.

The chart below shows maximum average daytime temperatures in Port Louis.

	J	F	M	A	M	J	J	A	S	O	N	D
°C	30	29	29	28	26	24	24	24	25	27	28	29
°F	86	84	84	82	79	75	75	75	77	81	82	84

Cyclones. The cyclone season is between December and April. Cyclones, powerful tropical storms, start hundreds of kilometres away to the northeast of Mauritius and take days to move westwards. Weather stations in the Indian Ocean track their route and warnings are broadcast days in advance. Cyclones vary in strength, some merely bringing heavy rains and winds, but others can have devastating effects, resulting in damage to buildings and cuts to the power and water supply. All hotels have their own generators and are well equipped to deal with a cyclone. When red warning flags are flown from public buildings you should not venture out. Local radio and TV stations broadcast regular bulletins. For cyclone information, dial 8996 from any Mauritian landline or 171 from a local mobile.

CLOTHING

Loose cotton shorts, shirts, T-shirts and dresses are ideal for the balmy climate of Mauritius. Men should wear a collared shirt and trousers at dinner in upmarket hotels; a jacket and tie is necessary only for formal functions. Wearing swimsuits in the hotel dining room or in town is likely to offend, while nudity and topless bathing on any beach is not permitted. A sturdy pair of walking shoes or boots is essential if you intend to go rock-climbing or hiking on the island.

CRIME AND SAFETY

Mauritius is a generally low-risk destination. Any crime that does take place is usually opportunistic, so avoid deserted, unlit places, wear a money belt if visiting Port Louis market, don't flaunt expensive jewellery and don't give lifts to strangers. If driving, never leave anything on show in your car and remember to lock doors and windows in self-catering accommodation. All hotels provide free safety deposit boxes. Do not leave money, jewellery, laptops or cameras on show when you leave your hotel room unattended, even for a few minutes. If you should become a victim of crime, report the details to the police immediately and insist on either a copy of the report or reference number for your insurance purposes.

Sadly, there is one 'no-go area', the slum settlement of Karo Kalyptus, just north of the capital, Port Louis. Motorists have been victims of nasty attacks when forced to slow down on the motorway at the adjacent Roches Bois roundabout.

D

DRIVING

Driving regulations. Drivers should be over 23 and must at all times carry an international or valid driving licence from their own country to avoid incurring a hefty fine. Drive on the left. Speed limits are 90km/h (60mph) on the motorway and 50km/h (30mph) elsewhere. Distances and speed limits are shown in kilometres and road signs are in English. The wearing of seatbelts is compulsory and there is no age restriction for front-seat passengers. Parking restrictions apply in towns and you should display a parking coupon, available in booklets from petrol stations. If you hire a motorcycle, you must wear a crash helmet. Accidents should be reported on an 'agreed statement of facts' form which is provided with your hire car. Personal-injury accidents must be reported to the police. Be warned: Mauritius has one of the highest road-death rates in the world due to badly lit streets, poorly placed road signs, an absence of decent pavements and incompetent driving habits.

I'd like to rent a car now/tomorrow for one day/a week **Je voudrais louer une voiture tout de suite/demain pour une journée/une semaine**
driver's licence **permis de conduire**
car registration papers **carte grise**
Fill the tank, please. **Le plein, s'il vous plaît.**
My car has broken down. **Ma voiture est en panne.**
There's been an accident. **Il y a eu un accident.**

Fuel. Most filling stations are open from 7am to 10pm but there are some open 24 hours on the motorway near residential areas. Prices for petrol and diesel are on a par with those in Europe. Petrol costs about R40 per litre. Attendants will fill your car and do not expect a tip. Ensure you have cash as credit cards are not accepted everywhere.

E

ELECTRICITY

Electrical appliances in hotels operate on 220 volts. Both square three-pin plugs and round two-pin plugs are used on the island, but take an adaptor.

EMBASSIES AND CONSULATES

Australia: Rogers House (2nd floor), John Kennedy Street, Port Louis, tel: 230 202 0160, www.mauritius.embassy.gov.au.

Canada: c/o Blanche Birger Company Ltd, Jules Koenig Street, Port Louis, tel: 230 212 5500, www.canadainternational.gc.ca/southafrica.

New Zealand: PO Box 683 Bell Village, tel: 230 286 4920, www.safe travel.govt.nz.

South Africa: 4th floor, BAI Building, Pope Hennessy Street, Port Louis, tel: 230 212 6925, www.dfa.gov.za.

UK: 7th floor, Les Cascades Building, Edith Cavell Street, Port Louis, tel: 230 202 9400. There is also an Honorary Consul in Port Mathurin, Rodrigues, tel: (230) 832 0120, http://ukinmauritius.fco. gov.uk.

US: 4th Floor, Rogers House, John Kennedy Street, Port Louis, tel: 230 202 4400, http://mauritiususembassy.gov.

EMERGENCIES (see also Medical care and Police)

The following numbers are useful 24 hours a day in an emergency:

Police **999**
Fire **995**
Ambulance **114**

G

GAY AND LESBIAN TRAVELLERS

Homosexuality is tolerated in Mauritius, but open displays of affection between same-sex couples may draw unwanted attention and catcalling.

GETTING THERE (see also Airport)

Most visitors arrive in Mauritius on a packaged scheduled airline deal provided by their home travel agent. Scheduled flights with the national carrier, Air Mauritius (www.airmauritius.com), come from Europe, Africa, Asia and Australia. Travellers from the US will need to take a connecting flight. Air Mauritius flies from the following destinations: London, Paris, Frankfurt, Munich, Vienna, Brussels, Geneva, Zurich, Madrid, Rome, Durban, Cape Town, Nairobi, Moroni, Harare, Antananarivo, Seychelles, Hong Kong, Singapore, Kuala Lumpur, Mumbai, Delhi and Perth. Fares from the UK start at around £5500.

The only way of getting to Rodrigues is by air or sea from Mauritius or the French island of Réunion. The flight takes about 90 minutes. From Mauritius, the sea voyage aboard the *MV Mauritius Pride* or the *Mauritius Trochettia* takes about 27 hours. Contact the Mauritius Shipping Corporation (tel: 230 217 2285) or your travel agent.

A French charter company, Corsair, flies from Paris to Mauritius, and other charter flights are destined to follow. An alternative is to book online at www.corsair.fr/flight/home. Other airlines serving Mauritius are: Air Austral (www.air-austral.com, British Airways (www.britishairways.com), Air France (www.airfrance.com), Emirates (www.emirates.com), Condor (www.condor.com), South

African Airways (www.flysaa.com) and Air Seychelles (www.air seychelles.com).

GUIDES AND TOURS

If you're staying in an isolated hotel and want to see the island, the best way is to book a guided tour. Tour operators, such as Mauritours (tel: 230 467 9700), White Sands (tel: 230 605 1500) and Summertimes (tel: 230 427 1111) have hospitality desks at major hotels and can arrange full- and half-day tours in air-conditioned vehicles with multi-lingual guides, as well as sea excursions, helicopter trips and other services. Smaller companies operate in the resort areas, but you should avoid freelance 'guides' on the beaches because they won't have appropriate insurance.

Air Mauritius Helicopter Section (tel: 230 603 3754) offers regular sightseeing tours. Prices vary depending on flying time and route. Current tariffs start at R13,000 per helicopter per two people (additional R4,000 per any additional person), which can accommodate up to four people. Transfers from the airport to your hotel for a maximum of four people are R22,000 per helicopter; see www.air mauritius.com/helicopterrates. Reservations for an airport–hotel transfer should be made before leaving home through your travel agent.

H

HEALTH AND MEDICAL CARE

Mauritius is malaria-free and no vaccinations are needed unless coming from an infected area. You should take out travel insurance, but remember that many companies exclude coverage for extreme sports, such as rock-climbing and mountaineering, although you may be covered for quad-biking. If you are contemplating taking part in any sea or land sports, confirm with the tour operator that the activity is within your level, keeping in mind that the operator is in business to make money. You should ask your guide to confirm that he or she is a qualified first-aider and that drinks and first-aid equipment are carried at all times. But most importantly – and this cannot be stressed enough – ask what emergency back-up measures exist in case of accident or sudden illness. Although emergency medical treatment is no longer free in public hospitals, these tend to be overcrowded and understaffed places, and ambulances are poorly equipped. If there is any doubt at all, don't book.

There are plenty of good private clinics that recognise overseas travel-insurance policies, so keep all receipts and documentation in the event of a medical claim. The cost of emergency and/or routine treatment is substantially less than in Europe. If you need a doctor or dentist consult your hotel. Most generic medicines are available at pharmacies, which are recognisable by a green cross, but if you are on any special medication it is better to bring your own.

Tap water is generally safe to drink, except during water shortages or cyclone periods, but in case of doubt there is plenty of bottled water available. Tummy upsets should be rare since food in hotels is prepared under strict hygienic conditions.

Wear protective shoes when exploring the reef and muddy waters. If you should tread on the venomous stonefish seek medical treatment immediately.

Public hospitals. SSR Hospital, Pamplemousses (tel: 230 243 4661); Moka Eye Hospital, Moka (tel: 230 433 4015); Doctor Jeetoo Hospital, Port Louis (tel: 230 212 3201); Princess Margaret Hospital, Quatre Bornes (tel: 230 425 3031); Jawaharlal Nehru Hospital, Rose Belle (tel: 230 603 7000). **Private clinics** accepting medical insurance are: Clinique du Nord, Tombeau Bay (tel: 230 247 2532); Clinique Darné, Floréal (tel: 230 601 2300); Med Point Clinic, Quatre Bornes (tel: 230 426 7777); Grand Bay Medical and Diagnostic Centre (tel: 230 263 1212); Apollo Bramwell Hospital (tel: 230 605 1000); and Centre Medical du Nord (tel: 230 263 1010).

LANGUAGE

The official language is English, although most people are more comfortable conversing in French. Creole, a form of pidgin French, remains the *lingua franca*. You'll also hear Indian and Chinese languages spoken, such as Bhojpuri (a sort of Creolised Hindi), Tamil, Urdu, Telegu, Marathi, Gujurati, Mandarin and Cantonese. Nearly everyone employed in tourism speaks both English and French.

MAPS

The tourist office produces a free map, and other reasonable ones can be found in hotel shops. The Government of Mauritius publishes the best map, which includes an insert of Rodrigues. In Mauritius it costs around R400 and can be bought in Port Louis at the Caudan Waterfront Bookshop, or the Ministry of Housing, Lands and Environment, 3rd Floor, Edith Cavell Street. An alternative is the French IGN No. 5/15. Both maps are also available in the UK at Stanford's, 12/14 Long Acre, Covent Garden, London WC2E 9LP, tel: 020 7836 1321, www.stanfords.co.uk.

MEDIA

For a country whose official language is English there are surprisingly few publications in English. What books there are tend to be imported and expensive, and current magazines and newspapers are often hard to come by. All local newspapers are in French and include *Le Matinal* and *L'Express*, which have some articles in English. The only English-language newspapers are *News on Sunday*, published on Friday, *The Independent* and the on-line paper *Newsnow*.

The top hotels provide satellite TV. The Mauritius Broadcasting Corporation (MBC) transmits television news in English at 9am and

9pm, and radio news at 8am, 3pm and 9pm daily. On radio, the BBC World Service is broadcast all day on 1575AM. Local radio stations focusing on pop music, interviews and items of local interest are: Radio 1 on 101.7FM, Radio Plus on 88.6FM and Top FM on 105.7FM.

MONEY

Currency. The currency used is the Mauritian rupee (R). Notes are in denominations of 25, 50, 100, 200, 500, 1,000 and 2,000; coins are R1, R5, R10 and R20 and 5, 10, 20 and 50 cents. There is no restriction on the amount of foreign currency you can bring in to the country, but if you have a surplus of rupees on departure you can convert them to your home currency. Keep all bank receipts as you can only export a maximum of R350.

Currency exchange. The rupee is a fluctuating currency, so keep an eye on the daily exchange rates. There are many banks in Grand Baie, Port Louis and at the airport, which offer much better deals on major currencies than in your hotel or through official money-changing shops.

> Do you accept traveller's cheques/ this credit card? **Acceptez-vous les chèques de voyage/cette carte de crédit?**

Credit cards. Major credit cards are accepted in large supermarkets, more expensive shops and restaurants, top hotels and car-hire companies. Many retail outlets display credit card symbols but always check that they accept your card before making any purchases. Some petrol stations do not accept credit cards at all. Be aware of high costs charged by your bank or credit card company when using plastic abroad.

Traveller's cheques. Most traveller's cheques in major currencies can be cashed at banks and hotels. Always take your passport with you.

ATMs. ATM's are found at banks, supermarkets and shopping malls.

O

OPENING TIMES

Shops: Shops in Port Louis are open weekdays 9am–5pm and Saturdays 9am–noon. In the plateau towns most shops close at noon on Thursdays. Port Louis Municipal Market is open Monday to Saturday 6am–6pm and Sunday 6am–noon. The small corner shops or boutiques are open daily 6am–6pm.

Businesses and offices: Weekdays 8am–4.30pm; some businesses are open Saturday morning 9am–noon. Government offices are open weekdays 9am–4pm, but close for lunch between 11.15am and noon.

Banks: Monday–Thursday 9am–3.30pm; Friday 9am–4pm. Closed Saturday and Sunday.

Museums: Hours vary greatly. Some close for one or two days a week and at weekends. Check before making a long journey.

Restaurants: Restaurants do not keep late hours and last orders should be made before 9pm. Many close on Mondays.

P

POLICE

Most police officers on Mauritius are friendly and keen to help visitors to the island. English is spoken at all police stations and there are specially trained tourist police in Grand Baie. Police Headquarters are at Line Barracks, Port Louis, tel: 208 0034; http://police.gov.mu.

The police generally leave tourists alone, but if you are driving always carry your licence in case of random checks. There is also a strong presence of police on the 'motorway' where speeding is common and offenders instantly reported.

Where's the nearest police station? **Où se trouve le commissariat de police le plus proche?**

POST OFFICES

On Mauritius, post offices are the only place where you can buy stamps and post letters. Registered parcels to overseas destinations are checked before being sent, so don't seal them until presenting them at the post-office counter. The price for sending a small postcard to anywhere in the world is R17 and to Europe is R15. Mail for other destinations should be weighed. Delivery normally takes between three and 10 days. Parcels received in Mauritius from overseas are always checked by customs and must be collected in person at Post Office Parcel Office, Quay Street, Port Louis, tel: 230 213 4813; remember to take your passport with you.

There are six post offices in Port Louis. The main post office is in Quay Street, tel: 230 208 0033 (www.mauritiuspost.mu). Post offices are open weekdays 8.15am–4pm; Saturdays 8am–11.45am.

PUBLIC HOLIDAYS

The following are public holidays when all public services are closed:
1 and 2 January New Year's Day
1 February Abolition of Slavery Day
12 March Republic Day
1 May Labour Day
2 November All Saints' Day
25 December Christmas Day
In addition, there are eight major festivals, mostly with moveable dates, celebrated by the various religions. The date of Eid ul Fitr, marking the end of Ramadan, varies from year to year according to the lunar calendar, and over time can take place in any month.
January/February Chinese Spring Festival
Mid-January/February Cavadee
February/March Maha Shivaratree; Holi
March/April Ougadi
15 August Assumption Day
Septembe Ganesh Chaturthi

October/November Divali
On Rodrigues, Chinese-run shops and businesses shut down for about one week during Chinese Spring Festival.

R

RELIGION

Just over half the population (52 percent) are Hindu, 31 percent are Christian, predominantly Roman Catholic, and some 16 percent practise Islam. Chinese faiths are also celebrated. Some religious festivals are also public holidays and reflect the religious tolerance of Mauritius's multicultural society. When visiting temples or mosques, remove your shoes and cover arms and legs. In Rodrigues the main religion is Roman Catholicism with most churches being in Port Mathurin (where there is also a Hindu temple and a mosque).

Services in English are held as follows: Roman Catholic Mass on Saturday at St Joseph's Chapel, Celicourt Antelme Street, Rose Hill (tel: 230 464 2944); Church of England service every Sunday at 8.30am (except the second Sunday of each month) at St Paul's Church, La Caverne, Vacoas (tel: 230 686 4819); Presbyterian service at St Columba's Church, Phoenix (tel: 234 7043 8888). On Rodrigues, St Barnabas Church in Jenner Street holds an English-language service once a month on Sundays at 8.30am.

T

TELEPHONES

Roaming services are available through Orange (www.orange.mu) and Emtel (www.emtel.com) networks who can also supply local SIM cards if you plan to stay longer. You will need to produce passport identification and wait at least one working day to be connected. The cheapest way to phone overseas on a conventional phone is to buy a pre-paid Sezam phone card and, for local calls, the Passe Partout or Emtel card. Both cards are widely available in units of R50, R100 and R200 (VAT included). As in the rest of the world, if you use your hotel phone you will incur hefty surcharges. Pay phones are cheaper to use from 10pm to 6am Monday to Friday, from noon to 6am on Saturday and all day Sunday. You can find phone booths taking cards and coins at police stations, post offices, shops and supermarkets. In Port Louis, there are telephone booths at Mauritius Telecom Offices at Rogers House, John Kennedy Street, or at Mauritius Telecom Tower at Edith Cavell Street. Both are open 8.30am to 5pm weekdays; Saturdays 8.30am to 2pm.

For international mobile phone rental, see: www.cellularabroad. com/rentals-mauritius.php. The international dialling code for Mauritius and Rodrigues is 230. To call home from Mauritius or Rodrigues, dial the international code 020, followed by the country code, the area code and the local number, omitting any initial zero.

Local numbers have mostly seven digits. Simply dial the number for connection. In case of difficulty or if you need directory enquiries, contact the operator on 150.

TIME ZONES

Mauritius is four hours ahead of Greenwich Mean Time (GMT).

New York	London	Jo'burg	**Mauritius**	Sydney
7am	noon	2pm	**4pm**	10pm

TIPPING

Tipping is not compulsory, but if you have received good service any tips will be appreciated. A service charge of 10 percent is normally included in restaurant bills; ask if you are unsure. Airport porters are not allowed to take tips. Taxi drivers do not expect tips.

Is service included? **Est-ce que le servis est compris?**

TOILETS

Public toilets have improved in recent years but there are still some pretty dire ones at bus stations and markets, which are to be used in emergencies only. Best of the bunch are inside the Caudan Waterfront complex in Port Louis and those found in big supermarkets and shopping complexes. Most public beaches also have adequate toilets. In emergencies you can always use the toilet in a café or restaurant. Carrying your own toilet paper is highly recommended.

TOURIST INFORMATION

Official tourist information can be obtained by visiting www.tourism-mauritius.mu. The Mauritius Tourism Promotion Authority (MTPA) has the following offices abroad:

Australia: Mauritius High Commission, 2 Beale Crescent, Deakin, Canberra, ACT 2600, tel: 061 2 6281 1203.

UK: 32–33 Elvaston Place, London, SW7 5NW, tel: 020 7581 0294.

US and Canada: Tourist information can be obtained from the Mauritius Embassy, Suite 441, 4301 Connecticut Avenue NW, Washington DC 20008, tel: (202) 244 1491/92.

In Mauritius the main MTPA office is on 4th floor, Victoria House, St Louis Street, Port Louis, tel: 230 210 1545. Tourist information centres are located at Trou d'Eau Douce Waterfront, tel: 230 480 0925; and inside the airport arrivals hall (tel: 230 637 3635). Rodrigues' tourist office is in Port Mathurin (tel: 230 832 0866, www.tourism-rodrigues.mu).

TRANSPORT

Buses. Buses are provided by dozens of bus companies, individual owners and co-operative societies. They are reliable, cheap and plentiful, even if some are rather dilapidated and slow. During the week they are crowded from 8am to 9am and 4pm to 5pm, but at other times, bus travel can be a pleasant experience and a way of rubbing shoulders with local people. There are two bus stations in Port Louis: Immigration Square (tel: 230 242 1425), serving the north, and Victoria Station (tel: 230 212 1174), serving the plateau towns and the south. Fares range between R20 and R50, or up to R100 if travelling by air-conditioned express service. Conductors will baulk at notes, so always carry small change. Queues are orderly and you buy your ticket on board.

Buses operate in the resorts from 6.30am to 6.30pm, elsewhere from 5.30am to 8pm, with the last bus leaving at 11pm from Port Louis to Curepipe via the plateau towns.

Taxis. Taxis are not metered. Although tariffs are regulated and a tariff card should be displayed it is customary to agree a price before accepting a journey. Licensed taxis can be hired from taxi stands in town and outside most hotels, or just ask your receptionist. The hotels have a special arrangement with the drivers, who are expected to charge reasonable rates. If you feel you are being overcharged, warn the driver that you will report him to the hotel. This strategy normally works.

Taxis are recognisable by black registration numbers on white plates. Avoid the unlicensed taxis (taxis marrons), which are instantly recognisable because they are nothing more than private cars that have white numbers on black plates. Rates may be low but they are not insured to carry passengers. Taxis can be hired for a full or half day and are often cheaper than hiring a car to drive yourself.

Taxicab Mauritius (www.taxicabmauritius.com) and Taxis Mauritius (www.taxismauritius.com) are reputable companies which display their rates online.

V

VISAS AND ENTRY REQUIREMENTS

Nationals of the EU, USA and all Commonwealth countries do not need visas. Your passport should be valid for six months beyond your arrival date. Entry is normally for a maximum of three months and you will be asked for your return or onward ticket and to provide an address in Mauritius. For longer stays you should go in person to the Immigration Department, Sterling House, Rue Gislet Geoffrey, Port Louis, tel: 230 210 9312. You will need two passport-size photographs, valid return tickets and evidence of funds to support your stay.

Firearms and ammunition must be declared on arrival. Prescription medicines for personal use carried in an official container are permitted. Finally, anyone trying to engage in drug trafficking is likely to find themselves in jail for a very long time.

W

WEBSITES AND INTERNET CAFÉS

There are a number of useful websites giving information for people intending to visit Mauritius:

www.pawsmauritius.org – animal welfare charity working to reduce the stray dog population by mass sterilization programmes.

www.mauritian-wildlife.org – for information on Mauritian fauna.

http://metservice.intnet.mu – the official meteorological site.

www.mauritiusgovernment.com – official government website.

www.mauritiusshipping.intnet.mu – for sailing schedules of MV *Mauritius Pride* from Mauritius to Rodrigues.

http://coronanorth.webs.com – social group for mainly female English-speaking expatriates.

www.newsnow.mu – online English language paper.

www.otayo.com – for what's on the local cultural scene.

www.islandinfo.mu – online magazine with local listings and map.

Internet cafés: Internet cafés are springing up in many tourist resorts and most towns on Mauritius. Rates for 30 minutes' surfing vary between R40 and R80. There are cyber cafés at the following locations:

Cyber 2000, Sivananda Street, Phoenix

Urbizz Ltd, Coastal Road, Flic en Flac

Cyberia, Wong Ching Building, Rose Hill

Click & Go, Astrolab Building, Port Louis Waterfront.

RECOMMENDED HOTELS

The most stylish accommodation is owned and managed by major Mauritian hotel companies, such as Beachcomber, Sun International, Indigo Resorts, Veranda Resorts and Naiade. A growing option is the all-inclusive stay, bookable through your home travel agent.

The following guide indicates prices for a double room with breakfast during low season. A higher price rating does not necessarily indicate that accommodation and service are superior, but has more to do with number of facilities and proximity and access to exceptionally well-maintained beaches. Locally known as *pieds dans l'eau* ('feet in the water') these properties command higher prices than those just a few blocks inland. Remember to add 15 percent vat when budgeting for your accommodation.

$$$$	over 15,000
$$$	R10,000–15,000
$$	R5,000–10,000
$	below R5,000

PORT LOUIS

Labourdonnais Waterfront $$$$ *Caudan Waterfront*, tel: 230 202 4000, www.labourdonnais.com. Port Louis' flagship business-class hotel, named after the founder of the capital, Bertrand François Mahé de Labourdonnais, hogs the best position on the waterfront. The tastefully decorated rooms have gorgeous mountain and harbour views. Open-door policy attracts non-residents to its three restaurants and elegant bar.

St Georges $$ *19 Rue St Georges, tel: 230 211 2581*, www.saint georgeshotel-mu.com. Unpretentious 60-roomed hotel in a quiet part of the city appealing to short-stay business and leisure travellers. The simple restaurant serves Creole and European fare.

Le Suffren $$$ *Caudan Waterfront, tel: 230 202 4900*, www.lesuffren hotel.com. Named after a French admiral, this 100-room hotel has a distinct nautical atmosphere, with swimming pool and artificial beach giving views over the capital. Trendy bar and á la carte restaurant attract a hip Friday-night crowd. Complimentary beach trips and water taxi to its sister hotel, the Labourdonnais.

THE NORTH

Le Palmiste $$ *Trou aux Biches, tel: 230 265 6815*, www.hotel-le palmiste.com. Popular with independent and tour groups. Pleasant, simple accommodation only five minute walk from the beach. Buffet restaurant and three pools; holistic treatments available in the spa.

Paradise Cove $$$$ *Anse La Raie, tel: 230 204 4000*, www.paradise covehotel.com. Small and luxurious retreat in a remote location overlooking Coin de Mire Island. Superb à la carte restaurant, spa and gorgeous private white beach. Popular with honeymooners. Dive centre.

Paul et Virginie $$ *Coast Road, Grand Gaube, tel: 230 288 0215*, www. veranda-resorts.com. All-inclusive option and authentic colonial atmosphere make this a firm favourite with Europeans. Two swimming pools, fine seafood and buffet restaurant, intimate bar and 81 comfortable sea-facing rooms.

The Oberoi $$$$ *Baie aux Tortues, Pointe aux Piments, tel: 230 204 3600*, www.oberoihotels.com. A small, elegant and highly sophisticated place, strictly the preserve of honeymooners and the occasional A-list celebrity seeking absolute calm. Superbly furnished individual villas, some with plunge pool and high-walled outdoor bathrooms, guarantee privacy. Open-sided silver-service restaurant overlooks a white sandy beach, and Balinese-style statues adorn two pools.

Trou aux Biches Resort & Spa $$$$ *Triolet, tel: 230 204 6565*, www.beachcomber-hotels.com. Closed for two years after major reconstruction this Beachcomber hotel is a village-style resort complete with villas and private pools and six restaurants. Good choice for honeymooners, empty nesters and families with young children.

Veranda $$ *Grand Baie, tel: 230 209 8000*, www.veranda-resorts.com. Warm tropical décor and stylish contemporary furnishings at this cosy ocean-fronted hideaway. Choice of 20 bungalows and apartments with kitchenette, plus 74 well-equipped standard rooms, poolside dining, mini-club for 4–12 year olds, tennis courts and sweeping views of the bay.

Villa Valari $ *Beach Lane, Morcellement Gexim, Preybere, tel: 230 5851 4162,* email: villavalari@gmail.com. The villa is Patrick and Marie's holiday home on the north coast. It is a comfortable and well-equipped place with a sense of being 'at home'. Situated not far from Mont Choisy and La Cuvette beaches.

Villas Mon Plaisir $ *Royal Road, Pointe aux Piments, tel: 230 261 7471*, www.villasmonplaisir.com. Charming family-run complex of two-storey units in pleasant gardens with pool situated on the edge of the village and right on the beach. Welcoming restaurant and bar. Free watersports and dive centre.

Zilva Attitude $$ *Royal Road, Calodyne, tel: 230 204 9800,* www.zilva-hotel-mauritius.com. In Creole, 'zilva' means 'islander'. The hotel was designed with the aim of sharing the simple and genuine life of islanders with its guests. The perfect place to just slow down and relax. Five themed restaurants offer delicious cuisine. Popular with families, couples and newlyweds.

THE EAST

Beau Rivage $$$$ *Belle Mare, tel: 230 402 2000,* www.naiade-group.hotels-in-mauritius.eu This is an eminently chic retreat appealing to honeymooners, couples and families. The bar and restaurant overlooks a gorgeous pool and beach. Wonderful spa, nightly entertainment, free watersports and mini-club for 3–11 year olds.

Belle Mare Plage $$$$ *Belle Mare, tel: 230 402 2600*, www.constance hotels.com. Large, well-established hotel that has benefited from regular refurbishment. Luxurious villas with private plunge pool or standard rooms are set in lush gardens with swimming pools and sea views. Free watersports, dive centre, mini-club for 4–12 year olds, two championship 18-hole golf courses, several à la carte restaurants and intimate bar provide everything you need for a beach-activity holiday.

Friday Attitude (formerly Hotel Bougainville) $$$ *Trou d'Eau Douce, tel: 230 402 7070 or 230 204 3820*, www.friday-hotel-mauritius.com. Go for the personal attention rather than a prestigious address at this all-inclusive haven where you can use the same beach as much grander hotels in the area. Newly furnished rooms, swimming pool, intimate restaurant and bar.

La Hacienda $ *Lion Mountain, Vieux Grand Port, tel. 230 263 0914*, www.lahacienda.mauritius.com. Situated in the historic region of Old Grand Port which offers several important historical sites. The property overlooks a large bay, the sea and outer islands. La Hacienda contains four unique guest houses, surrounded by private gardens with both mountain and sea views.

Long Beach $$$$ *Belle Mare, tel: 230 401 1919*, www.longbeach mauritius.com. Contemporary urban themes in this piazza-style beach resort with restaurants, shops and bars sheltered behind natural sand dunes. Hotel interchange scheme with sister hotels, Le Touessok, Sugar Beach and La Pirogue.

Le Preskil $$$ *Pointe Jerome, Mahébourg, tel: 230 604 1000*, www. lepreskil.com. Superb location with views of Lion Mountain and Île aux Aigrettes Nature Reserve. Popular with groups, being only a 15-minute drive from the airport. Garden rooms and sea-facing cottages in warm colours contrast with a trio of powdery white beaches.

THE SOUTH

Le Domaine L'Arbre du Voyageur $$ *Tamarin Falls, Henrietta, tel. 230 291 2946*, www.ledomainedelalarbreduvoyageur.com. Simple log cabins in rural setting ideal for exploring walking trails in Black River Gorges. Opportunities for hunting and horse riding. Rustic restaurant and bar. Children welcome.

Les Ecuries de la Vieille Cheminee $$ *Chamarel, tel: 230 483 4249*, www.lavieillecheminee.com. High in the Chamarel mountains and close to the Coloured Earths, these charmingly rustic self-catering chalet bungalows offer a chance to explore rural Mauritius. There are opportunities for horse-riding and trekking, as well as dining in nearby village restaurants. A two- or three-day stay here makes an unusual alternative to the usual sun, sea and sand.

Heritage Awali Golf & Spa Resort $$$$ *Bel Ombre, tel: 230 266 9777*, www.heritageresorts.mu. Lots of in-house activities and free shuttle trips to nearby nature reserve and golf course compensate for the isolation of this luxury hotel. Distinct Creole-African theme with large thatched-roof restaurants and bars, two fine pools and mini-club.

Heritage Le Telfair Golf & Spa Resort $$$$ *Bel Ombre, tel: 230 266 9777*, www.heritageresorts.mu. This unique masterpiece of grand colonial-inspired architecture transports guests to an atmosphere of elegance and calm. Rooms have floor-to-ceiling windows with private balconies. Luxuriant gardens, five restaurants (one with show kitchen) and bars, spa, mini-club and unlimited golf. Guests can alternate between swimming in the lagoon and exploring the undulating hills of the Bel Ombre Nature Reserve.

Sofitel So Mauritius $$$$ *Royal Road, Bel Ombre, tel: 230 605 5800*, www.sofitel.com. Definitely a 5-star experience. A fantastic oasis boasting lush vegetation and a beautiful lagoon.Thai architect Lek Bunnag's project here was enhanced by the designs of Kenzo Takada. Elegant and truly sophisticated, with attentive service. Well-being and spa service available.

THE WEST

Maradiva Villas Resort & Spa $$$$ *Wolmar, Flic en Flac, tel: 203 403 1500*. www.maradiva.com. Sprawling complex of luxurious suites set in tropical gardens overlooking long stretch of beach. Fine dining options, kids' club, spa and short taxi ride to bars and restaurants at Flic en Flac.

Le Paradis $$$$ *Le Morne Peninsula, tel: 230 401 5050*, www. paradis-hotel.com. Le Paradis is a haven for beach and nature lovers that includes international celebrity sportspeople on its guest list. As well as bars and restaurants, the resort includes a championship 18-hole golf course, and offers deep-sea fishing, scuba diving, mountain biking, mini-club for 3–12 year olds and lively nightly entertainment.

Sands Resort $$$$ *Wolmar, Flic en Flac, tel: 230 403 1200*, www. sands.mu. Discreet, serene and sophisticated beach hotel with wonderful views of the Tamarin Mountains. Ideal for empty nesters and honeymooners. Fine restaurant and huge swimming pool.

Sugar Beach $$$$ *Wolmar, Flic en Flac, tel: 230 403 3300*, www.sugar beachresort.com. Cool, white and spacious hotel reminiscent of colonial times, but with all mod cons. Particularly lively at night when entertainment shows are held around the swimming pool. Enjoy a drink in the palatial 19th-century-style sugar plantation manor house. Guests can also use the restaurants at the adjacent sister hotel, La Pirogue.

Tamarin Hotel $$ *Tamarin Bay, tel: 230 483 3100*, www.hoteltamarin. com. Nightly entertainment by local musicians and singers attract jazz lovers from far and wide. Close to the village and a great location for body surfing. Facilities include a cinema, mini-club, Zen spa, long rectangular swimming pool for serious swimmers, a surf shop and a boathouse.

Villas Caroline $$ *Coast Road, Flic en Flac, tel: 230 453 8411*, www. villa-caroline-hotel-mauritius.mu. Attractive, well-maintained complex overlooking a brilliant white spit of sand within walking distance of restaurants and bars. Superb dive school and a wide range of water sports.

PLATEAU TOWNS

Gold Crest $$ *Route St Jean, Quatre Bornes, tel: 230 454 5945*, www. goldgroupofhotels.com. Comfortable, long-established 59-room hotel popular with short-stay visitors and those looking for an inexpensive town base. Convenient for shopping, and there are plenty of buses to Port Louis and Flic en Flac beach.

Henessy Park Hotel $$ *65 Ebene Cyber City. tel: 230 403 7200*, www. hennessyhotel.com. Formerly Link Ebene City Hotel, now under new management. Contemporary business-class hotel with gym, pool and coffee shop. Lively clientele at weekends in the alfresco bar. Convenient access to Port Louis.

RODRIGUES

Cotton Bay Hotel $$$ *Pointe Coton, tel: 230 831 8001*, www.cotton bayhotel.biz. Comfortable billet in superbly isolated beach location. Great diving right on the doorstep and access to some glorious walks.

Escale Vacances $$ *Fond La Digue, Port Mathurin, tel: 230 5772 9303*, www.escale-vacances.com. Stay in a cosy family atmosphere only a five-minute walk from the centre of town at this Creole-style hotel, which has an excellent restaurant.

Morouk Ebony $$ *Pate Reynieux, Port Sud-Est, tel: 230 832 3351*, www.mouroukebonyhotel.com. Attractive bungalow-style accommodation in cliff-top location with boathouse, dive school and kite surfing.